Saddlery
and Horse Equipment

Showjumper Melanie Smith (USA) rides *Calypso*, who is fitted with a plain cheek snaffle bit, Flash noseband and running martingale; forward-cut jumping saddle with simulated sheepskin numnah and Atherstone girth; and over-reach (bell) boots and open-fronted leather tendon boots on his forelegs.

A PRACTICAL HORSE GUIDE

Saddlery
and Horse Equipment

Jennifer Baker

ARCO PUBLISHING, INC.
NEW YORK

Published by Arco Publishing, Inc.
215 Park Avenue South, New York, N.Y. 10003

First published in Great Britain in 1982 by
Ward Lock Limited, London, a Pentos Company

Library of Congress Cataloging in Publication Data

Baker, Jennifer.
  Saddlery and horse equipment.

  Includes index.
  1. Saddlery. 2. Horsemanship—Equipment and
supplies.
3. Horses—Equipment and supplies. I. Title.
SF309.9.B34 1982   685′.1   82-11468
ISBN 0-668-05633-9

Printed in Great Britain

Acknowledgements

Front jacket photograph by David Johnson.
Back jacket photograph by Bob Langrish.
**Saddlery and equipment for front jacket photograph
kindly lent by Swaine Adeney Brigg and Sons Ltd, of
Piccadilly, London.**
Line diagrams by George Thompson.

Photographs by Bob Langrish, pages 2 and 61; Parker
Gallery, pages 6 and 93; Mary Evans Picture Library, pages
9 and 10; John Elliot, page 18; George Parker and Sons,
page 27; Society of Master Saddlers, page 29; Peter
Roberts, pages 70, 73, 74, 75, 76 and 77; 'Kiwi' Rugs, page
85; other photographs by the author.

Contents

Tack for hunting in 1738. The slope of the saddle encourages
the rider to sit towards the back. The bridle has no noseband.

Introduction – history and development of saddlery

Man's first use of the horse was as a food animal. Primitive hunters killed the horse by driving him to his death over the nearest cliff, or bombarding him with rocks. Later, by using his hide, the hunters invented the *bolas*, a contraption of three stones inserted in hide bags and linked together with hide thongs, which they hurled at their prey to entangle the legs and so bring the animal to the ground, where he was clubbed to death.

Some 5000 years ago the horse was domesticated and used for milk, transport, communication and war. Initially he was used as a pack animal and probably in draught, pulling a primitive form of sledge similar to the *travois*, an arrangement of two poles attached at one end to the horse and dragging along the ground at the other, the intervening area covered probably with skins to form an area on which loads could be pulled. This was certainly used by the American Indians hundreds of years later.

In around 1800 BC, long after the invention of the wheel, there is evidence of the horse and ass being used in chariots, and carts, with harness adapted from the yoke used for the ox. This type of harness continued for some 2-3000 years, until the horse collar was invented, which enabled the full use of the horse's pulling power to be made.

The first evidence of the horse being ridden is in engravings on the tomb of Horenhab of Egypt *circa* 1600 BC. Whether the animal depicted is a horse or an onager (an animal whose domestication preceded that of the horse) is debatable; but the horseman is pictured sitting bareback on the rump of the animal and controlling him by use of what we now know as a snaffle bridle.

There follows further evidence showing horsemen in the East riding small, Arab-type horses. The 14th century BC Syrians were using a well-developed form of bridle, although still no saddle. The Assyrians, who followed in around 890-824 BC, had rather more sophisticated equipment and had devised a more elaborate bridle. They had also developed the forerunner of the saddle, a decorated padded cloth without girth or stirrups, which was kept in place by a breastplate.

During the 6th century the Persians became the leading horsemen of their time, and a rather heavier type of horse came into general use. Evidence shows them to be universally overbent and wearing snaffle bits with straight cheeks, and it is a safe assumption that the nosebands were spiked as are the Spanish *caretas* which are still in use. Attempting to evade them, horses tucked their noses in. Emphasis, too, was gradually being placed on stronger bits; and by the 4th century BC, the Celts of Gaul had developed a curb bit. This trend continued and the Greeks and Persians developed stronger and sharper variations on the same theme, incorporating rollers and spikes.

Meanwhile, the Scythians, an interbred race of Iranians, Mongol Turks and Huns who lived in the remote plateaus of the Ukraine, used a plain jointed snaffle with long, straight cheekpieces and had developed, sometime during the 5th century BC, the first padded leather saddle. This consisted of two hide cushions stuffed with horsehair and joined in the middle with a leather strap across the spine. This was then placed on the saddlecloth and the rider's weight was thus placed evenly across the back either side of the spine.

With the coming of Xenophon in 430-355 BC, a new era of equestrian knowledge materialized. It was he, for instance, who recommended attaching 'short lengths of chain to the mouthpiece for the horse to pursue with his tongue' and by so doing encouraged the horse to play with and accept the bit; this was, of course, the forerunner of the keyed mouthing bit. It was Xenophon, too, a Spartan cavalry officer, who encouraged his troops to jump across country. Although he appreciated both the instability of jumping without the aid of a saddle, (while despising saddle cloths for their insecurity) and also the difficulty of cavalry charging in the battle field without parting company with the horse at the moment of impact, it was not until some 700 years later that the wooden saddle was developed. Xenophon's calvalry, however, relied heavily on javelin throwing rather than close combat, and for this a degree of collection was necessary. Although true collection could not be achieved without the aid of the curb, which he did not use, Xenophon understood the need to get the hocks well underneath the horse and achieved this to a surprising degree.

Roman equipment of the second century was as likely as not copied from that of the barbarian *foederati*, which supplied the Roman Cavalry arm, and shows a development of the saddle cloth which is fitted with padded rolls at front and rear. But it is likely that the Sarmatians developed the wooden raised base covered in leather hide or cloth, raised at both cantle and pommel to keep the rider in place, and it was these same people who excelled at the charge, holding their lances underhand for maximum effect. At a similar time, however, the 'X-Group' of Africans (whose remains have been found in the Nile Valley) were also using a saddle, high at pommel and cantle and often decorated with silver, although both they and the Sarmatians were still stirrup-less. The 'X-Group' about whom very little is known, had also developed a ring bit which comprised a rounded, jointed snaffle mouthpiece which en-

circled the jaw, the two ends culminating in one ring behind the jaw to which the reins were attached.

Considering how long it took to develop the saddle, the stirrup followed very quickly and was known to be used by the Mongolian Huns of Attila. In no small measure, this simple device, originally made of rope, was responsible for the destruction of the Huns' opponents. It was much easier for a soldier to shoot the enemy down in a rain of arrows if he was standing in the stirrups, and it also meant that he could ride faster and further without tiring. Others soon saw the advantage the stirrup gave and copied it, gradually replacing the rope with leather and then metal.

The Middle Ages saw the emergence of the armoured knight and the Great War Horse, the armour becoming heavier to shield the knight from arrows, and the horse in consequence becoming heavier and bigger. This trend continued until after the Battle of Crecy in 1346 but this battle was probably the turning point for the heavy horse and armour, and a lighter and more refined form of riding and horse soon became popular, resulting in the development of tournaments and jousts.

This required a high degree of collection and precision riding which is epitomized in the classical equitation of the Renaissance period of the 1500-1600, when riding became acknowledged as an art form. Riding halls abounded in Europe and the system of progressive training spread throughout the continent, the emphasis being placed on breaking the horse's resistance. The spiked noseband was again in evidence although in theory at any rate some consideration was given to 'preserving the mouth'.

Following a dark spell, when barbaric items such as iron bars, rods, goads and even cats and hedgehogs tied to the horses' tail were used to bend the horse's will, a more enlightened age placed more emphasis on suppling horses by 'more natural and less mechanical means'.

The saddle for manège riding was padded and again made with high pommel and cantle, while the bitting arrangement consisted of a curb, either with or without a port and with very long cheeks, often as much as 12-15in (30-38cm). The leverage on these was enormous, and pro-

Horse and rider of 1450 in full armour, in France.

Illustrations from the Duke of Newcastle's book, *New method of horsemanship*, 1743.

duced the very overbent position so beloved of that period, although Federico Grisone (who started the first riding school in Naples) placed great emphasis on a 'good mouth'.

Antoine de Pluvinel ran a riding school in Paris in the early 17th century, and was a rather more enlightened student of horsemanship, appreciating that all horses are individuals and treating them as such. But his main claim to fame was the 'pillars' which are still used in the Spanish School today. A young horse was tied to the pillars, one on each side, by ropes attached to the cavesson and in such a position that with the aid of an appropriately placed whip the horse could be taught to perform the *piaffe*, *levade*, and other high school movements. With the rid-

den horse, however, Pluvinel's chief aid was the use of the sharp spur, which had been developed during the Middle Ages when heavily-encased knights needed 'an extra leg' in order to be able to reach the horse's flanks.

It was not until the 18th century that the 'Father of Classical Equitation', François Robichon de la Guerinière, emerged. He was a disciple of Pluvinel and his influence has extended to the present day; his teachings include the high school airs which the Spanish Riding School in Vienna claims to have perpetuated.

At this time horses were not, however, reserved totally for manège riding. Hunting, in England at least, had its followers too, notably Henry VIII who was a keen follower of the buckhounds. The vastly overbent head carriage and a high degree of collection were not required across country and a freer carriage was preferred, snaffle bits being used, although the straight-legged position of the manège riders was still adopted.

The classical form of riding continued in Europe through to the 19th century, when military riding, based on the classical school, took over. Little thought, however, was given to jumping until an Italian cavalry officer, Federico Caprilli (1868-1908), realized that cavalry could be most effectively used if it could gallop at speed across country and thus be used for reconnaissance. This included jumping anything that came in its way.

This thinking developed into the 'forward system' which required horse and rider to acquire free natural balance under all conditions, and the rider to sit foward in the saddle using a shorter leather, insisting that he must be positioned over the moving centre of balance.

The general-purpose seat adopted today for pleasure riding is a compromise developed from the forward system and the classical method, and it can be seen how the different uses to which the horse has been put over the centuries has necessitated a changing type of equipment. It is this saddlery which in turn affects the horse's performance, and it is important, therefore, to understand the function and construction of saddlery if we are to make the best possible use of the horse's potential.

1 Saddlery and Horse Anatomy

A badly-fitting saddle will be uncomfortable for both horse and rider and will, because of the discomfort felt by the horse, result in a poor performance and lack of free forward movement. Conversely, a horse who is comfortable will be able to use himself more freely without any fear of being pinched. In order to understand how the saddle should fit correctly, so as to help rather than hinder performance, it is first necessary to consider the skeleton and muscle formation of the horse and how he moves.

Skeleton

The frame or skeleton is made of bone and the bones are held together by ligaments which allow movement to go so far and no further. Any damage to ligaments leads to lameness, as the movement of the joints to which they are attached will have become impaired. The junction of two bones is known as a joint. To prevent the bones grating on each other and wearing down, the ends of these joints are covered by layers of gristle known as cartilage and surrounded by fluid called joint oil or synovial fluid.

Muscles cover the whole of the skeleton, and being formed of an elastic-type substance, allow the horse to move by virtue of the tendons which are attached to the bones at one end and the muscle at the other. Again, if a tendon becomes damaged or strained, the horse will suffer a greater or lesser degree of lameness, depending upon the severity of the strain, as the joint to which it is attached will not be able to move correctly. The elastic property of the muscles allows the limbs to stretch and contract to the same degree, thus motivating the activity of the joint.

The main group of muscles concerned with the topline of the horse are those which are arranged in pairs and run from the neck down either side of the spine and its covering, the cervical ligament, right down to the croup. The cervical ligament is responsible for the horse rounding his back and producing the necessary propulsive thrust from the hindquarters, but it can only do this if the horse is encouraged to stretch his head and neck, thus forcing a degree of tension in the back. The dorsal muscles on each side of the spine are important when the horse moves on anything but a straight line, the muscles on one side of the animal stretching when he turns a corner and the corresponding muscles on the other side contracting accordingly.

Contrary to popular belief the spine does not flex throughout its length, but only in the area between the last of the dorsal vertebrae and the first of the lumbar vertebrae. In a short-backed horse, therefore, there is virtually no flexion, whereas a horse with a slightly longer back will in consequence have slightly more flexion. The horse's spine, possibly because of the way it lies in the womb, is not entirely straight, and much of the training of the horse is designed to increase the flexion as much as possible in this area; this is aimed at making his efficiency greater by positioning the propulsive thrust of the quarters directly behind the forehand instead of to one side.

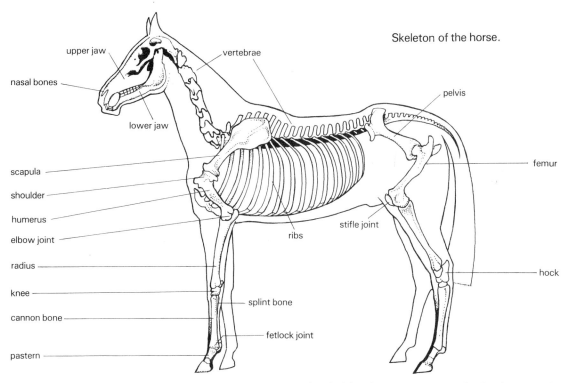

Skeleton of the horse.

upper jaw

nasal bones

lower jaw

vertebrae

pelvis

scapula

shoulder

humerus

elbow joint

radius

knee

cannon bone

pastern

femur

stifle joint

ribs

splint bone

fetlock joint

hock

A short back denotes strength but tends to be uncomfortable, since the full force of the hindlegs coming under the body is felt by the rider sitting in the saddle; but a long back, although more comfortable, tends to be weak although mares are permitted (in official standards) to have longer backs than geldings.

The diagram of the skeleton shows that there is a very thin covering over the vertebrae of the wither, back, loins and croup, and that since there is no form of support to the body mass in the area of the back, this is the weakest part of the body and that least suitable for carrying weight. It is, however, the only place upon which to sit; and any deformities in this area, such as a hollow back or its opposite, a roach back, make saddle fitting difficult and increase the possibility of damaging the vertebrae.

A hollow back can be caused by the trainer of a young horse insisting on a 'correct' head carriage before the horse has been allowed to stretch his head and neck, thus stretching the cervical ligament and the attendant muscle structures. If this raised head carriage is imposed before the horse has been built up and

schooled in the correct way, the back can only hollow, and the hindlegs, instead of being brought underneath the body as required for propulsive movement, will be pushed out behind the body and be useless as a propulsive power.

Movement

Basically the horse is a rectangle with a weight supported by a pole, his head and neck, at one end; the whole being supported by four pillars, his legs. The centre of gravity of this rectangle is, at rest, positioned slightly to the rear of the withers and approximately half-way down the horse's body. The animal's weight, however, is not distributed evenly over all four legs, rather more weight being put over the forelegs than the hindlegs. When the horse moves, his balance and his distribution of weight moves according to the speed at which he is travelling; the faster he moves the further forward his centre of gravity moves, while in collected paces the centre of gravity shifts further back. The rider's weight, to remain in balance with the horse and not

13

Horse with rider at centre of balance at rest, in the lowest part of the saddle, hips square with the horse's, the spine vertically above the horse's.

inhibit his movement, must be kept directly over the horse's centre of gravity. Obviously a horse with a heavy head and thick neck will carry more weight on the forehand, and a horse with the opposite attributes will have his point of balance shifted correspondingly further back. A rider sitting out of balance, either too far forward or too far back in the saddle, will, in addition place more weight either over the forelegs or the hindlegs.

Most sore backs are caused by pressure of the saddle on the spine and friction on the muscles when the horse is unfit; but a large heavy rider who has not learnt to ride and who bumps about in the saddle will find that his horse has a sore back within a very short space of time.

To ensure that the muscles on either side of the spine are developed equally it is important that the rider frequently changes his diagonal at the trot. There are differences of opinion as to whether one should sit on the inside or outside diagonal when riding a circle (the inside diagonal on a circle is when the near-fore and off-hind come to the ground together, and the outside diagonal is when the off-fore and near-hind

reach the ground). The important thing, however, as far as the horse is concerned, is that the diagonal should be changed even when riding in relatively straight lines, as otherwise the horse will become used to carrying the weight of the rider on one side of his back, and developing the muscles on that side accordingly; while the muscles on the opposite side will not receive the same stimulus for development. The result will be a horse who is stiff on one side, or onesided, the exact opposite of what one is aiming for.

Saddles

The basic purpose of a saddle is to make sitting on, and riding a horse more comfortable for the rider, at the same time giving him greater security and therefore more control over his horse. A good, modern saddle will, in addition, help the rider to sit over the horse's point of balance and thus keep in balance with the animal.

The modern saddle made with a deep seat, full panels, sloping head and knee or thigh rolls, is a variation on that used by the Italian riding teacher and innovator, Caprilli (1868-1908) at

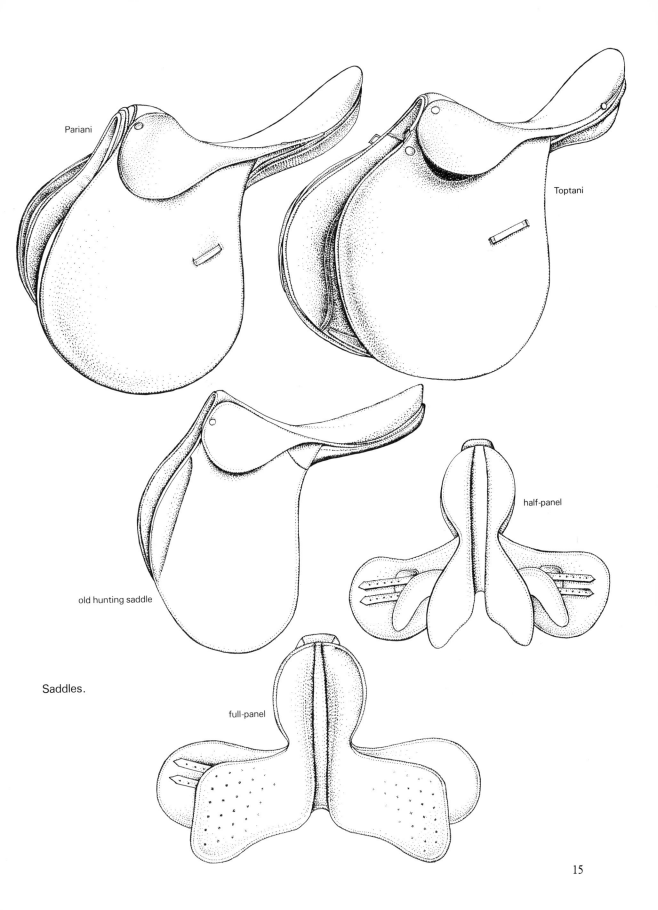

Pariani

Toptani

old hunting saddle

half-panel

full-panel

Saddles.

15

the beginning of this century. This was in turn a variation of that used by the American jockey, Tod Sloane (1874-1933) who revolutionized the racing world of his time by adopting a forward, crouching position and placing his weight forward, thus freeing the horse's loins and hindquarters, unlike his contemporaries who sat back and behind the movement.

The first saddles marketed along the lines of Caprilli's teachings were those made by Pariani of Milan, Italy, in the 1920s, and this same firm was the first to make a spring tree saddle. A spring tree is one that has two strips of tempered steel inserted into an otherwise rigid tree, running lenthwise, which has the effect of allowing the saddle to 'give' to the movement of the horse's back and the rider's seat.

It was a pupil of Caprilli's, Piero Santini, who was responsible for the 'Santini' forward-position saddle being made in Britain, at Walsall. This, together with the 'Distas', designed by Jack Hance and F.E. Gibson, and the 'Danloux', made in France by Hermès, was the first of the modern saddles.

The old English hunting saddles were built on a hand-made beechwood tree and initially had a full serge-lined panel and straight flaps. Later a half panel was introduced, known as a Rugby panel, since it was in that town, in Warwickshire, that the panel was first used at the turn of the century, when Rugby was a centre for polo. Whilst it was easy for the saddler to manipulate the wool stuffing in a serge-lined saddle, serge did tend to absorb sweat from the horse, and later linen was used as a lining.

The old hunting saddle, by having a shallow seat and a high pommel, caused the rider to sit back, virtually over the horse's loins, restricting the horse's action and contributing to a hollowing of the horse's back; the modern saddle is different, and places the rider in the centre of the saddle. The knee or thigh rolls support the thigh above the knee. The stirrup bars are recessed and placed under the tree instead of on top as in the old hunting saddles, and are positioned further forward than of old, thus enabling the stirrup leathers to hang further forward and the rider's leg consequently to be placed in such a position that it can be used to maximum effect, rather than being stuck out in front.

This modern saddle, therefore, contributes to the rider having a deep seat, and by positioning him as closely to the horse as possible and fixing the leg, gives support, security and maximum control.

Bridles

The object of the bridle is to provide a means whereby the bit can be attached to the horse's mouth at one end and the rider's hands at the other. The purpose of the bit is to help in controlling the speed and direction of the horse, by assisting the rider to place the head in the correct position. However, it must be remembered that the bit is only an extension of the rider's hand at the end of the rein, and no bit will produce the desired result on its own.

As with saddle fitting, the horse must first be sufficiently schooled and fit before any attempt is made to place the head in the required position. Initially, the horse must have the cervical ligament stretched so that his neck becomes supple and he can round his back sufficiently to get his hocks underneath him, since all movement starts from behind.

Once he is in this suppled state a bit can be placed in his mouth; and there are five main groups of bits from which to choose, each with its own specific action, as explained in Chapter 3. These are: snaffle, double bridle or Weymouth, Pelham, gag, and bitless bridle. The snaffle is the one most commonly used for ordinary riding. In the show ring the double bridle comes into its own, while the Pelham seems to find favour with children; and the gag and bitless are seen most frequently in the show-jumping arena, although the latter can be used when there is any sort of mouth injury.

There are, too, many accessories which are dealt with in detail in Chapter 5; some accentuate and others completely alter the purpose of particular bitting arrangements. For instance, a standing martingale is designed to prevent a horse from raising his head above a certain level; but it is frequently seen in use with a double bridle, which is designed to achieve a relatively high head carriage.

Whatever bit is used, however, the fact that it must fit the horse's mouth is of paramount

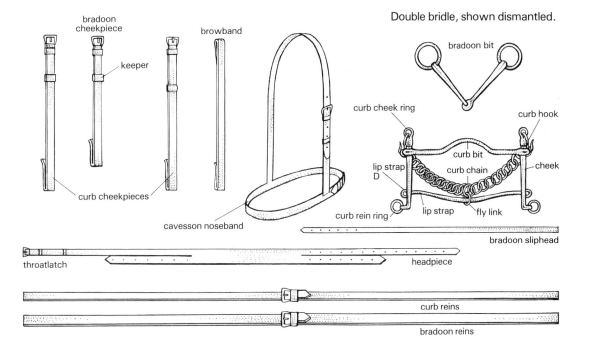

Double bridle, shown dismantled.

bradoon cheekpiece

browband

keeper

bradoon bit

curb cheek ring

curb hook

curb bit

lip strap D

curb chain

cheek

curb cheekpieces

lip strap

fly link

cavesson noseband

curb rein ring

bradoon sliphead

throatlatch

headpiece

curb reins

bradoon reins

importance. A bit that is adjusted too low in the mouth, so that it comes into contact with the teeth, will be uncomfortable for him and will positively encourage the horse to get his tongue over the bit; whereas one that is too narrow will pinch the corners of the mouth. If the horse is not comfortable in his mouth he will not be able to perform and go forward freely and happily. The same applies to the bridle, where particular care should be taken to see that the browband is not too tight and his ears do not get pinched.

Saddlery materials

The horse world is basically a conservative one and tends to stick to the old-established, proven ways; but new materials do appear on the market from time to time. Leather, of course, is the material from which tack and harness is traditionally made, but plastic and nylon have been used with success for certain items of tack and clothing in recent years.

Nylon is used extensively for the manufacture of girths and headcollars, the girths being made in the same way as the string ones which were popular many years ago. Nylon headcollars (halters in USA) have become very popular, especially for use on ponies. They are, of course, very much cheaper than leather ones and are particularly suitable for use on ponies who are turned out in the paddock during the day, but who are difficult to catch. If the pony rolls and gets the headcollar wet and muddy these conditions do not affect the nylon as they would leather, and it can, of course, be easily washed.

Driving harness is an expensive item of equipment and nylon webbing breast-harness has proved popular in some areas, especially with donkey driving enthusiasts; and again the cost is very much lower.

Plastic has proved a popular alternative to leather in making the various boots used for horses, and brushing boots and tendon boots, for instance, are now frequently made of plastic. These boots obviously get very wet and muddy especially when used in deep going and they are very easy to wipe clean, without having to be dried off and oiled. 'Velcro' (quick-release) fastenings for these boots have to some extent replaced the traditional buckle fastenings and

17

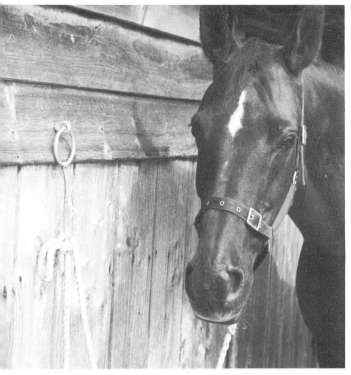

An adjustable nylon headcollar ensures comfort and a secure fit, besides being durable in wet weather.

again it makes fastening quick and easy, and 'Velcro' is also used extensively on stable and travelling bandages in place of the traditional tapes; some horses dislike the noise it makes, however, until they are accustomed to it.

Nylon simulated sheepskin material is used a great deal in the making of numnahs. It is cheaper than sheepskin and easily washable but in some instances it can cause the horse to sweat up under the saddle. Padded foam numnahs covered in heavy cotton material are probably more satisfactory.

Perhaps most advancement in the way of new materials has been made in actual horse clothing. Stable rugs (blankets in USA) based on the nylon, quilted jacket or anorak have appeared on the market as an alternative to the traditional jute night rug. Made of quilted nylon and filled with polyester fibre, they have either brushed nylon or cotton linings and are both very light and very warm. Cotton linings are considered preferable. Another revolutionary new fabric to be used for stable rugs is 'Thermatextron' which is again very light, has a high thermal insulation and absorbs less moisture than other material. 'Equitex' fabric rugs give a hard-wearing outer surface whilst maintaining their flexibility and comfort, and are lined with brushed polyester.

New Zealand rugs, and in particular those classed as 'All Purpose' rugs, i.e. ones that the makers claim be worn in the stable or paddock, have also benefited from modern materials. Strong, waterproof synthetic material lined with acrylic fibre pile is the order of the day for several rug manufacturers, the pile lining being detachable in some cases. (*See* Chapter 8.)

The main advantage of all these modern materials, in the case of both tack and clothing, is that they are all easily maintained, being washable, are easy to put on, light, and, in the case of clothing, very warm. Ease and speed are today's bywords and the horse world can't opt out entirely.

2 Materials, manufacture, care and maintenance

The leather process

Leather is the basic material used in the making of saddles, bridles and other tack and harness. Fundamentally it is animal skin which has been chemically treated to preserve the skin's natural qualities. Most of the leather used in the saddlery trade comes from cattle, but pig, sheep and deerskin are also used for specialist items. In Britain a great many of the hides required for the making of saddlery are produced there, the best hides coming from youngstock, and Aberdeen Angus cattle are considered to supply some of the best hides. However, a great deal more is imported since Britain cannot meet the heavy demand of the saddlery and leather trade; and the greatest proportion of this used to come from Argentina and now from parts of Europe, N. and S. America and Australia. All hides are imported either in their natural state, or after being tanned but before the currying, or finishing, process has been carried out, since Britain prides itself on having the best craftsmen for this work.

Before it can be used the hide has to be removed from the animal and treated. As in all animals the skin is divided into three layers; the outer layer, the epidermis, which consists of the hair, cells and glands; the middle layer, the corium, which is composed of tough fibres and fatty cells which holds together the inner and outer layers; and the inner layer, the flesh, which is composed of cells, which holds together the skin as a whole and the muscles.

After removal from the carcass the hides are then soaked in drums containing lime and other chemicals in order to loosen the hair and the outer layer of skin. The inside flesh layer also has to be removed, either by machine or with the use of a special knife, and the remaining epidermis and corium are then soaked in further lime and bacteria solutions which remove any further unwanted matter. The hair is removed next, either by scraping it with a special knife or by machine, and the hides are then soaked again, this time in an acid solution, in order to remove the lime left by previous soakings. Finally, the hides are subjected to scudding, i.e. the removal of any bits of remaining hair, tissue and dirt etc and this is done by hand using a special blunt knife with the hides hung over a beam. The hide is then thoroughly washed before being tanned.

Tanning prevents the hide decaying. The process was probably discovered by accident in prehistoric times, animal skins being left out in the forest where the rain-soaked tree bark and leaves accumulated in puddles and combined to form tannic acid. Tannic acid is still very widely used in the curing process, and it leaves the leather any shade from light brown to a reddish brown. The hides are initially immersed in a weak solution of tannic acid, and gradually, over several months, they are moved into stronger solutions. Small hides are sometimes put in revolving drums of this same liquid, which reduces the amount of time necessary for them to be left.

At the end of the 19th century tanning, in order to produce stiff white chrome leather, involved the use of chromium salts, but this is little used today, although oil tanning or 'chamoising' is still used in some instances and is a variation of the old way of preserving skins by rubbing animal grease into them.

Today fish oil is used instead of animal grease and the hides are squeezed dry after washing and then pounded in special machines for several hours before being sprinkled with fish oil and pounded again. This performance is repeated several times before the skins are left in the drying room, where the oxidation of the oil and air produce the required chemical reaction to make the skin imperishable. Hides are then washed again to remove excess oil.

We are then left with the useful part of the skins or hides, and these are passed to the currier, who applies the colour and impregnates the leather to make it flexible, hard wearing and water resistant. The leather is now referred to as having two sides, the flesh side, which is the underneath, and the grain side, which is the outside. It is the grain side that has the colour added to it and is sealed and made virtually waterproof. Currying is carried out mainly by hand, a mixture of tallow, cod oil and other greases plus wax being thoroughly rubbed into the leather several times over a period of time; the hides, once processed in this way, are left to mature for some weeks before being used.

There are three main colours in which leather is produced, of which the most common is the golden yellow colour known as London colour. Havana, a darker shade, 'the colour of a good cigar', is also popular and both of these tone down with use and cleaning; but the third colour, Warwick, is much darker and tends to turn black with use. Warwick is often used in the making of driving harness, as opposed to riding tack. Those saddlers specializing in tack for the ridden horse used to be known in London and Walsall (the two principal British towns of the leather industry), as 'Brown Saddlers', whilst those specializing in harness were known as 'Black Saddlers'. The colour is produced by staining with aniline dye, usually by hand.

Whatever the colour it is important that the leather has sufficient substance, or thickness, to it, since, with the increased grease content, this will prolong its life and flexibility; and this is in no way affected by the colour. The degree of substance required does, however, depend on what item of equipment is being made. A fine show bridle, for instance, will not need as much substance as a thicker everyday hacking or hunting bridle, since it will not get the same degree of wear; but neither will it last as long. Similarly the flaps of a show or dressage saddle will not have as much substance as a general-purpose saddle, since the flaps are thinner in the former in order to put the rider as close to the horse as possible, and consequently they will not last so long. It is also important that the flesh side is smooth with no loose fibres, the leather be firm and slightly greasy and that the leather should fold naturally when bent without forming any bubbles on the surface.

Selecting hides for use

Hides are sold to the saddler either whole or in sections, as in the diagram, depending upon the item he wants to make. The butt, that section of hide on either side of the backbone, is the most suitable leather for saddle flaps and bridles. When extra long reins are required, as in driving harness, the full back, i.e. from the neck to the tail of the animal is used, although because the tendency has been for cattle to be killed younger in recent years, before they are fully grown, the extra length required is often difficult to obtain. The lower down the butt you go the poorer is the quality and substance of the leather, and the belly itself is too thin for anything other than odd straps and so forth. The shoulder is used mainly for headcollars, being thick and not so pliable as the butt. It is also cheaper and is often used for saddle flaps in poor quality saddles.

Saddle seats are made principally from pigskin since it has little substance, much elasticity, strength and wearing qualities. The grain side butt of the cowhide used for the flaps is embossed by pressing it with an engraved hot plate, to produce bristle marks characteristic of pigskin, so that it matches the seat. Cowhide flaps are sometimes covered with pigskin but in this case the cowhide must be thin if the resultant flaps are not to be very thick and rigid. Doeskin is also used on occasions, although it is very expensive, in the same way and if this is used the seat is also made of doeskin. Some saddles have suède thigh rolls and this can either be made of doeskin or ordinary cowhide, the grain side fluffed up to produce a suède nap. Sheepskin (basil) is used for lining cheaper saddles.

Rawhide is cowhide which has been specially tanned, leaving a white line through the centre of the thick hide. It is very strong and is frequently used for stirrup leathers and girth straps. It is frequently confused with the red-coloured ox or buffalo hides, made from the butt of those animals. Red ox and buffalo hides are used extensively for stirrup leathers since they are very strong, virtually unbreakable, and are specially treated to retain their tensile strength, since it is desirable that stirrup leathers do not stretch. Another leather often confused with rawhide and buffalo or ox hide is Helvetia leather which is again very strong, but is of a yellowy colour and is used mainly for lining and strengthening some nosebands and martingales. Girths are usually made of cowhide, and the girth straps, if not made of rawhide, are often made of chrome leather.

Metals

Metal is required for the production of bits, stirrup irons, buckles, curb chains, spurs etc. At one time they were all hand forged from steel, and beautifully made and finished, often being chrome plated. They did however rust, which is something that today's models do not do. The manufacturer of these metal items is traditionally known as the loriner.

Nickel is the cheapest of the materials used today but it is very unsatisfactory since it is easily broken or bent by simply knocking it against a hard object. It also turns yellow very quickly and needs to be frequently cleaned with metal polish in order to stay clean and bright. There are also nickel mixture bits, of which the best known are Kangeroo and Eglantine (used less), which are more expensive but neither rust, turn yellow nor, except on rare occasions, break.

Stainless steel is undoubtedly the metal most used today. Although it is the most expensive it is also the best. It does not rust nor discolour and is virtually unbreakable. Brass is used for the buckles on high quality headcollars and this too is very strong and does not rust; although frequent polishing is necessary if it is to stay

clean and bright, the look of a well-polished brass mounted headcollar is worth the extra effort. The only other metal used in the making of saddlery is aluminium, and since it is very light in weight it is used for stirrup irons and bits used in racing. It is not very strong however, and its only advantage is its lack of weight, so it is not suitable for ordinary riding equipment.

All metal items today are cast in a mould and then finished and polished by hand. The exception to this rule is the stirrup bars, which although on cheaper saddles, are cast, on the better quality saddle the bars are always made of forged steel, the words 'forged' or 'cast' being stamped on the bars.

Construction of the saddle

THE TREE

The shape of the saddle is determined by the framework, the tree, on which it is built, and ideally the tree should be built to fit the back of the horse for whom the finished saddle is intended. This, of course, is rarely possible and most saddles of a certain size and shape will fit most backs of the equivalent size and shape. Trees are usually made in three width fittings: narrow, medium and broad and four lengths: 15 inches (38 cm), 16 inches (40.6 cm), 16½ inches (42 cm) and 17½ inches (44.5 cm). The aim of the saddle tree maker is to produce a lightweight item which is at the same time a strong one. Craftsmanship and design have improved over the years to such an extent that the saddle has become a more simple item of manufacture, and unnecessary weight has been eliminated in the process.

Traditionally the saddle tree is made of beech-wood, but modern materials include plastic and fibreglass, both of which are very light and are consequently sometimes used in the construction of racing saddles. More widely used today, however, is laminated wood which is bonded together under pressure and formed in a mould. It has proved very successful, being both stronger and lighter than beechwood.

Whichever material is used, however, it has to be reinforced with steel plates which are placed on the underneath of the tree from the head to the cantle. Steel plates are also secured above

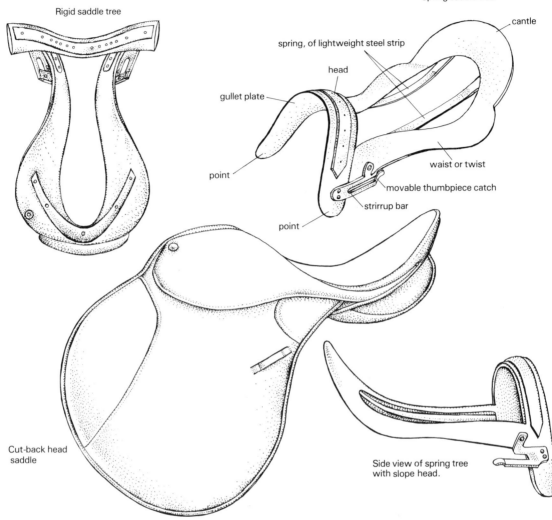

Saddle trees.

Rigid saddle tree

Spring saddle tree

cantle

spring, of lightweight steel strip

head

gullet plate

point

waist or twist

movable thumbpiece catch

strirrup bar

point

Cut-back head
saddle

Side view of spring tree
with slope head.

and below the pommel at the head and gullet of the tree. There are two principal designs of tree in the modern saddle – a rigid tree and a spring tree – the latter having a dipped seat while the former is more or less straight.

The spring tree

As the name implies, the spring tree has two 'springs' made of lightweight steel strips inserted into the underneath of the tree running from front to rear along the widest part of the seat, and set about 2 in (5 cm) in from the outside. This makes the seat more comfortable for the rider and provides more 'give' so that pressure from the rider's seat can be more easily transmitted to the horse, an aid which is used for various movements in a more highly trained horse. The spring tree saddle sometimes has a more sloped-back head while the rigid tree head is set almost vertical. Cut-back heads, as opposed to sloping heads, are also produced, usually, but not exclusively, being found on rigid tree saddles. They are useful for a horse who has particularly high withers when an ordinary head might press on that part of him. Otherwise they serve no purpose and become merely a fashion; but are today quite popular. Cut-back heads can be made with varying degrees of the head cut away in a sort of half-moon shape, from quarter cut-back to full cut-back, the term depending on the amount cut away; but, for all but the most pronounced withers, the sloping spring tree saddle head will satisfy.

Stirrup bars

Stirrup bars are attached to the tree below the head on the point of the tree. On the spring tree saddle they are set further forward than on the rigid tree, a position necessitated by the design of the tree head. They are also frequently, but not always, set recessed on the underneath of the point of the tree to avoid causing bulk under the rider's thigh, and this tends to be more comfortable. The bars are made in two pieces: the main bar on to which the stirrup leather hangs and a catch fitted at the unattached end. The thinking behind this gadget is that when the stirrup leather is in place the catch is pushed upwards so that the leather cannot slip out, but if the rider falls, leaving a foot in the stirrup iron, the catch comes undone and releases the leather thus preventing the rider getting dragged. In practice this does not work unless one happens to fall at just the right angle for the catch to be released, and it is very much safer to ride with the catch permanently open and a sufficiently large and heavy pair of stirrup irons so that the foot can slip out easily if the rider falls.

THE SEAT

The tree itself is covered in skrim, a sort of tough muslin cloth, and then has a black type of pitch painted over it in order to make it waterproof. Over the coated tree pre-strained strips of wide web are stretched and fastened tightly with small nails from the head of the tree at the pommel to the cantle, and over this is strained and nailed a piece of stretched canvas. This then forms the base of the seat. Around the widest part small pieces of leather are then added to round off the seat. A piece of serge is then tightly stretched and stitched down to the canvas layer to make the shape of the seat and in the middle of this a small slit is made so that wool can be stuffed down into the intervening space to make the seat more comfortable and to prevent the wooden tree being felt through the various layers by the rider. Cheaper saddles can be produced by eliminating the serge lining, the adding of leather pieces round the seat and the stuffing with wool and replacing the canvas with stretched jute; the leather seat being fastened on the top. As with all short cuts, however, this may possibly be false economy since the saddle

will not be nearly so comfortable, will not keep its shape so well, nor last so long.

The finished seat is put on next, and as mentioned earlier, pigskin is the leather most usually used for saddle seats because it is thin, elastic and durable. It should be put on when it is damp and stretched tightly so that when it dries and shrinks very slightly a neat, tight seat is produced. Doeskin, if used on the seat, should also be applied in the same way; and in Europe calf skin is frequently used, which is cheaper than either pigskin or doeskin but does not last so long. The saddle flaps, made of grained cowhides, are then stitched and nailed into place on to the tree and the skirts also added before the panels are fitted; the girth straps are stitched on now or before the saddle flaps.

THE PANELS

The panels of the saddle are the modern equivalent of the two cushions used by the Sythians. Their purpose is to give a comfortable padded surface to the horse's back whilst raising the tree sufficiently high to give easy clearance of his spine, and at the same time spreading the rider's weight over a wider area of back, thus avoiding pressure points.

Panels come in four shapes, the oldest, and that traditionally used in the old hunting saddles being the full panel, which is stuffed with wool and quilted, and covered in either leather, serge or linen. Leather is the most satisfactory lining but also the most expensive, and serge and linen have been used satisfactorily although are not so frequently seen today. Serge tended to be difficult to clean and absorbed sweat, resulting in the stuffing becoming lumpy. Linen, although satisfactory and easy to clean when used over serge, tended to crease up when used on its own. On occasions felt was used as a stuffing and this too proved very satisfactory requiring the minimum of attention since, unlike wool, it did not become lumpy. Although wool stuffing is still used today, plastic foam is now most widely used, since like felt it requires the minimum of attention and is in addition, very light.

Half panels were also used on the old hunting saddles but had their forte for use on children's ponies. Both full and half panels were used in conjunction with a rigid tree, and the half panel had additional sweat flaps, i.e. small pieces of thin leather which came about half way down the saddle flap and were about 6 in (15 cm) wide, fitted underneath the girth straps. The disadvantage of both the full and half panel saddles lies in the width at the waist of the saddle. They were considerably wider than the modern saddles and must have stretched children's thighs considerably.

The two remaining panels are both of a continental European pattern, one originating in France at Saumur and the other in Germany. One of them is used in the construction of most modern saddles. They are very similar in concept, both being narrow at the waist and with the whole panel being cut much further forward than in either of the other panels. These panels are not stuffed throughout and are almost always lined with leather. The underneath of the seat is, of course, padded and this padding is continuous through to the underneath of the panel and down the front of the panel thus forming a knee roll. The German pattern has in addition a thin thigh roll at the back of the panel, which besides ensuring that the leg stays in the right place, prevents the girth straps from slipping back too far.

Cleaning saddlery

REGULAR ROUTINE

Like anything else in constant use, saddles, bridles and other items of tack and harness become wet, muddy and dirty and because the horse wears these items next to his skin the sweat and grease from his coat gets on to the tack. In order to keep tack in good condition, therefore, it has to be cleaned regularly, after daily use, if the life of the leather is to be a long one. Leather that gets wet and hot, due to sweat from the horse's body, or is neglected, will become stiff and hard as a result of losing its fat content; the less substance it has to start with, the less it has to lose and the quicker the leather will deteriorate. In order to put this fat back into the leather, saddle soap and one of the proprietory greases or oils must be applied regularly and the latter is particularly necessary if the tack is being stored and not in regular use.

Before being cleaned saddles should be stripped, i.e. have the girth, buckle guards, stirrup irons and stirrup leathers, collectively known as 'furnishings', removed. A saddle will be easier to clean if it is placed on a saddle horse, i.e. a shaped wooden or metal stand, or bracket on which the saddle fits. When the 'furnishings' have been removed, a sponge soaked in cold or luke warm water, then squeezed out so that it is damp, should be rubbed over the whole saddle to remove all dirt and grease. Even if particularly dirty, hot water should not be used, neither should the leather be soaked since this will remove the natural oil content of the leather. Stubborn little lumps of grease and dirt, known as 'jockeys' tend to accumulate under the flaps and these should also be removed. If they do not come off by rubbing hard with a sponge they can be scraped off with a finger nail, but sharp objects which may cut the leather should never be used.

Leather should be left to dry naturally after sponging and on no account should it be put near a radiator or fire to dry as this will dry out the natural oil content. When dry, saddle soap should be applied to all parts of the saddle. Saddle soap is obtainable either in tins, or more usually now in bars which contain glycerine. This should be applied with a dry or very slightly damp sponge and the best effect is obtained by spitting on the bar of soap, rubbing the sponge on to it, and then rubbing the soap into the saddle using a circular motion until a shine appears on the leather – i.e. 'spit and polish'. On no account should the sponge or soap be wet enough to work up a lather as this will mitigate the soap's effectiveness.

Particular attention should be paid to the underneath of the flaps and skirt as this is the flesh side of the leather i.e. the side that has not been sealed and waterproofed and is therefore open to receive the soap's nutrient value. Stirrup leathers from which the irons have been removed, buckle guards and the girth, if it is a leather one, should all be cleaned in the same fashion. Stirrup irons, after removing the rubber treads (stirrup pads) if they are used, should be washed and dried and these together with the rest of the furnishings should then be replaced, remembering to run the irons up the leathers and laying the girth over the top of the seat, or if

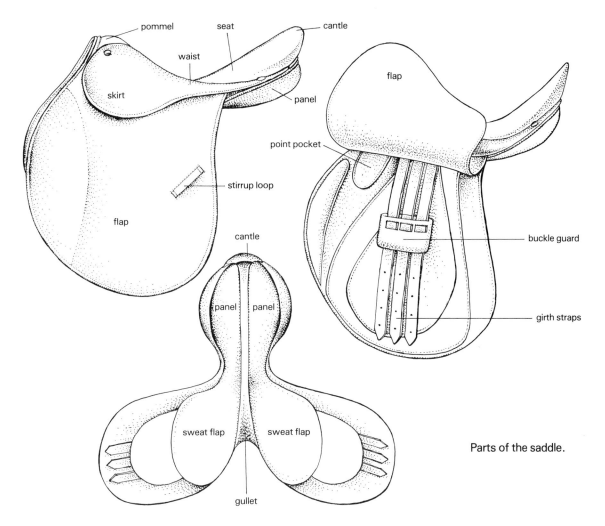

pommel

seat

cantle

waist

skirt

panel

flap

point pocket

stirrup loop

buckle guard

flap

cantle

girth straps

panel   panel

sweat flap   sweat flap

gullet

Parts of the saddle.

not for immediate use, hanging the girth and leathers straight down on hooks. Because the near-side leather stretches with use through mounting, it is a good idea to change the leathers over regularly.

If the saddle panel is made of linen instead of leather, this should be sponged clean ensuring that it does not become too wet, and if made of serge it should be brushed hard to remove hair and sweat. If the girth is made of Lampwick it should be scrubbed clean and dried, and the leather fastenings cleaned in the normal way and not allowed to become too wet. Care should be taken to see that the buckles are dried properly so they do not rust. Nylon girths should be brushed daily to remove mud, grease and hairs,

and washed when necessary with soap, drying away from direct heat.

Bridles should be dismantled completely, all buckles and billets being undone, before being cleaned, but remember, when undoing the buckles, which hole to put the strap back on to. Each piece should be cleaned thoroughly in the same way as the saddle, again paying particular attention to removing the jockeys and to rubbing in the soap on the flesh side. Like the stirrup irons the bit should be thoroughly washed, paying particular attention to the joint in the mouthpiece if the bit is jointed. If the reins have rubber along them this should be washed but not soaped. The leather parts should then be soaped. Take particular care to clean and soap

25

round the inside of the folds and round the billets or buckles.

KEEPING LEATHER OILED OR GREASED

Several times a month all leather items should be well oiled or greased to keep them supple and in generally good condition, and this can be done after the normal washing but before applying the saddle soap. There are a number of preparations on the market, divided into the grease and oil varieties. Generally speaking grease is better since oil tends to ooze out of the leather and too much of it tends to rot the stitching, whereas grease, particularly when applied to the flesh side, has the same effect without the messy after-effects. Neatsfoot oil, however, is a favourite preparation to use on new leather to darken it down quickly and it should be well rubbed in, especially in to the flesh side, and if not used in excess it is perfectly satisfactory.

New tack should always be oiled or greased before being used in order to make it supple and comfortable for both horse and rider. Among the grease varieties Koechoelin and Flexalan are probably the most popular in Britain and are equally good. Mink oil lotion is popular in the USA. When greasing tack do remember to coat the buckles and metal fastenings as well, particularly if the tack is being stored away for any length of time, and when storing it is as well to wrap the leather in an old pillowcase or something similar. Remember, too, to store tack in a dry room and never in a damp atmosphere if the tack is not to go mildewy. If bridles are to be stored, hung up, remove the bit first since the weight of the bit hanging down from the cheek-pieces will stretch the leather. The saddle should always be placed on a rack when not in use so that the air can circulate under the panels (*see* page 48).

Boot polish tends to be used on harness and headcollars in some cases, but this practice is not to be recommended since polish tends to seal the flesh side of the leather and in time makes it hard.

CHECKING FOR WEAR

At least once a month all tack should be checked for wear; and repairs, if they are necessary, should be carried out immediately by the saddler. Stitching in particular should be checked regularly, since this is usually the first thing to break, often with dangerous results. The most usual items to suffer from stitching coming undone are the reins, stirrup leathers and girths, so particular attention to these is vital. The bit should be checked regularly, too, to make sure there are no sharp edges and that the mouthpiece has not worn too thin.

Although there are many saddlery shops throughout the country, not all of them are willing to undertake repairs of anything other than a minor nature; the principal reason is that unless the shops have their own workshops on the premises and the craftsmen to do the work, it makes it an expensive undertaking as well as a time-consuming one if items have to be sent away, and customers are not always willing to pay high prices for repairs. So you may have to search when larger repairs are needed.

The saddlery trade

Up until the beginning of the 19th century, when nothing had changed drastically over the previous several hundred years and horses still provided virtually the only form of transport, the horse was probably responsible for providing more work than any other single commodity. The roads, particularly in big cities, were filled with coaches and carriages causing just as many traffic problems as today. In London the streets were filled with Livery and Bait Stables and markets selling food and bedding, of which the principal one was the street we still know as the Haymarket. There were 'Repositories for the Sale of Horses', notably Tattersalls of Knightsbridge, which sold the better class horse, and Aldridges and Beavers in St Martins Lane, which dealt in less blue-blooded equines.

Hatters, tailors, whipmakers, wheelwrights, coachbuilders, collar- and harnessmakers, bridlemakers and saddlers had constant employment, the carriage and harness trade reaching its peak at the beginning of the 1900s. The Coachmakers and Harnessmaker's Company had, however, received its first charter in 1677 and the Saddlers Company had been in existence since Anglo-Saxon times, the present Saddlers'

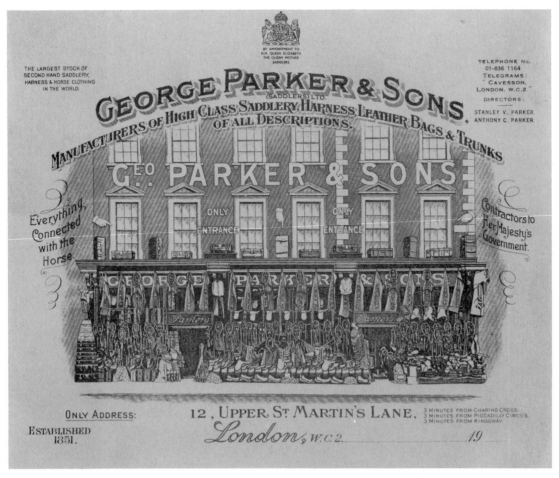

A view of the saddlery firm of George Parker and Sons, early this century.

Hall in Gutter Lane, off Cheapside, being the fourth to have been built on that site. Collarmakers were regarded as being at the lowest end of the scale, just above harnessmakers, but even at this low level they were expected to stitch 12-14 stitches to the inch (2.5 cm) on coachharness, with four rows of stitching on the traces for the princely sum of 7d.-8d. (approx 3½p.) per hour! The apprenticeship period was seven years and this resulted in highly skilled craftsmen being turned out. But if the wages were low so was the price of the end product, and up to 1914 a child's saddle could be bought for 50s. (£2.50) while a top quality saddle complete with stirrup leathers, irons and girth cost 5gns. (£5.25). By 1939 the cost had risen to 12gns. (£12.60).

The earliest established saddlery firm in Britain was Wilkinson and Kidd. They started business in 1786 in Hertford Gardens, and when their original building was pulled down in 1866, moved to 5 Hanover Square. They were sold in 1901, on the death of the founder, to Henry Wilson and moved to Oxford Street, before finally closing down. Blackwells also had premises in Oxford Street in 1796, then moved to Orchard Street and were sold to Champion and Wilton in 1893. Just prior to the Second World War, Champion and Wilton also took over Whippy, Steggall and Co, saddlers who were established in 1786 in North Audley Street; but Champion and Wilton were themselves taken over by W.H. Giddens (now in Clifford Street,

27

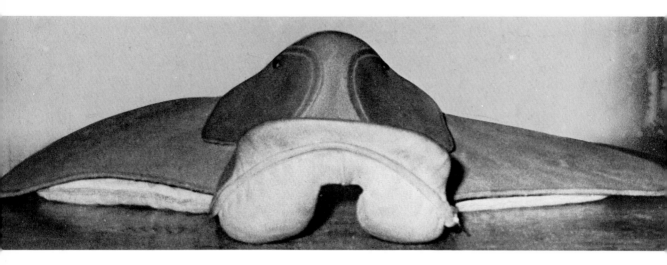

Example of a cheap Indian-made saddle, Note the unequal padding which would cause pressure and a sore back for the horse.

off New Bond Street), in 1961. Three years earlier Giddens had taken over McDougall who had themselves taken over Owen and Co, a company who had had premises in Mount Street, Grosvenor Square at the turn of the century and specialized in hunting and racing saddles. J.I. Sowter were taken over by Harry Hall (now in Regent Street) in 1967; and Eldrid Ottaway was established in 1751 and merged with Bliss before this firm was merged with Eldonian Brookes; they still manufacture saddlery at Walsall. Many other companies were either merged, blitzed during the Second World War, or concentrated on other areas of the leather trade such as the manufacture of luggage and handbags, or closed down entirely. Others, like William Jenkinson and Co, originally in the City, moved out of London, this firm combining with Matthew Harvey and moving up to Walsall.

The exception is George Parker and Sons which was established in 1851 in Little St Andrew Street, now renamed Monmouth Street, and moved to its present premises in Upper St Martins Lane at the beginning of the century. At one time three shops all selling saddlery were being run by different branches of the Parker family at the same time: Parker Bros, Parker and Parker, and George Parker and Sons, but today only the latter still exists.

BUYING NEW SADDLERY

While the bench-made London saddles are still probably the best in the World, there are now, since the resurgence of interest in the horse, small saddlery boutiques to be found through the length and breadth of Britain. The better ones buy their goods from Walsall, still the centre of the saddlery trade, and because they do not have the overheads of the London saddlers can sell their products somewhat cheaper. The worst ones buy their goods from less reputable dealers, pick them up cheap at markets and sales or sell imported Indian-made saddlery. These 'shops' can, of course, sell their tack at 'bargain' prices but you only get what you pay for, and it is false economy to buy this type of tack since the leather will be of very poor quality, will rarely fit the animal for whom it is intended and will frequently break after little use, and these shops are not then interested in providing the after-sales service to repair the equipment. Neither do they have the technical knowledge or ability to fit tack to the animal in question.

The top saddlers will be willing to come out to the owner's home to fit tack, particularly saddles, to the animal, but it is a service requiring knowledge and expertise and as such must be paid for. When buying a new saddle, however, it is the best action to take and they will also provide after-sales care in the way of repairs, stuffing saddles etc. A number of these saddlers also have a good selection of second-hand tack for sale; particularly with saddles, because new ones need 'breaking in' over a period of time, they can usually be a good buy, as they can be put to full use immediately.

Most but not all good reputable saddlers in Britain will be full members of the Master Saddlers' Association, who 'have skilled employees or are skilled in their own right in the manufacture, repair and maintenance of saddlery and harness and sell such goods by retail'. These firms will display their membership plaque or badge and since they can be relied upon to sell good quality products this is probably the best place to go to buy new tack. Most manufacturers fix a small metal plate with their name on to the saddle above the stirrup bar.

Tack can, of course, be bought from markets, but this is rarely satisfactory, since there is no come-back on the vendor if it does not fit.

BUYING SECOND-HAND SADDLERY

Frequently tack is sold 'with the pony'. If the pony comes from a private, knowledgeable home then for the novice this is probably one of the best ways of purchasing tack, since the previous owner will have ensured that the tack fits the pony in question and that it will have been cared for and maintained. However, there are unscrupulous owners about and it may be that the owner is trying to get rid of useless tack on unsuspecting buyers, so try to take a knowledgeable person with you when purchasing. See that the stitching and leather are in good condition.

The saddle should be tested to see if the tree is broken. Naturally if it is, the saddle should not be used. A good saddler can usually repair a rigid tree, but not a spring tree. If the cantle will bend forwards and backwards the tree is broken. To test further, hold the pommel towards you

The badge of the Society of Master Saddlers.

with both hands on the cantle and try to pull the cantle towards you gently; an unbroken spring tree saddle will flex across the waist and seat and will feel as if it is going to spring firmly back into place; a broken one will feel soft and lacking in spring, and may give more on one side than the other. A broken rigid tree will move on one or both sides.

If the front arch is broken, it will be low on the horse's back and may touch the point of the withers. To test for a broken arch, put a protective cloth on a smooth surface and place the saddle upside down on it; press down with one hand on each panel, over the point pockets; then press all over the inside of the saddle; then put the saddle the right way up with the seat between the knees and push inwards towards the tree from outside the flaps. Listen for any clicking or squeaks, and note any movement; both suggest that it is broken, and the saddle should be checked by a saddler.

3 Bridles and Bits

Bridles

There are five component parts of the bridle which are the same whichever type of bit is used. The various parts are: the bridle **headpiece** (crown piece), to which are attached the cheekpieces, and which incorporates the throatlatch. The throatlatch keeps the bridle from slipping off over the horse's head, should he, for instance, stop at a fence and the rider go over his head still holding the reins. The throatlatch should be adjusted so as to let the width of two to four fingers be easily inserted between it and the horse's throat. If it is adjusted too tightly it could throttle the horse; it would prevent him flexing at the poll and getting a collected head carriage.

The **browband**, through which the headpiece is slotted, keeps the latter from slipping back, and it is important that this is of the correct size, since one that is too small will push the headpiece forward and pinch the ears.

The **cheekpieces** or cheekstraps are buckled on to the headpiece at one end and fastened on to the bit at the other, usually by means of a metal billet, sometimes a buckle, of which more later.

The **noseband** has a long strap which passes through the headpiece and buckles back on to the shorter strap, and without it the horse looks virtually undressed. Ordinary cavesson nosebands should be adjusted so as to lie approximately two fingers below the cheekbones, and buckled to allow two fingers inside.

The **reins**, each fasten on to the bit, usually, again by means of a billet, sometimes a buckle, and buckle on to each other in the middle.

The bridle is, of course, made of leather and the five component parts are virtually standard for everyday riding. There are, however, numerous variations in reins and nosebands.

REINS

A plain leather rein is that most usually seen. There are others, however, among the most popular being the rubber-covered leather rein which has the advantage of giving a good hand grip in wet weather and when riding a sweaty horse. Reins are usually 5 ft (1.5 m) in length and the rubber covering starts approximately 10 ins (25 cm) from the bit and extending for some 30 ins (76 cm). The rubber is stitched along its length by hand or machine, the closer the stitching the less strong the rein will be. In due course the rubber will wear thin and probably split but it is a simple job for the saddler to replace it.

Leather plaited (braided) reins and laced reins are other variations. Both of these give a good grip, but may stretch with use, plaited ones more. Plaited reins are, as the name implies, strips of leather of either five or three strands – plaited together, whereas laced reins consist of an ordinary leather rein with a thread of leather passed at intervals through the rein in a v-shape.

Reins are not only made of leather, however. There are, for instance, nylon plaited reins made in many different colours along the same lines as the leather plaited ones. Nylon reins do, however, tend to be very slippery when wet and can be very hard when dry. Lampwick or web reins, however, are much more satisfactory and are very comfortable to hold. Most, but not all, of them are fitted with little strips of leather at intervals round the reins to prevent the reins slipping through the fingers. All non-leather reins do have leather at each end for attachments to the bit at one end and at the other end where they buckle on to each other or they can be one piece.

Rein attachments

Reins can be attached to the bit in a number of different ways, the most popular of which is by the use of a metal stud billet fastening (hook-in stud fastenings in USA). This is most usually seen in the form of a hook but it can also be a round stud. The loose end of the rein is passed through the bit ring, then back through the first keeper over the stud fastening, which is on the inside of the rein, and on through the second keeper. It is a very neat form of fastening and one that is simple to undo for ease of cleaning, and it makes changing the bit an equally simple affair. It is also a very safe form of fastening, the billet very rarely coming undone.

A variation of this billet is the snap billet which used to be used extensively on show bridles and was used particularly by that doyen of the show ring in Britain, Count Robert Orssich, on his prizewinning hacks. It is now, however, rarely seen. It is similar to a dog clip, the hook being attached to the cheekpieces and reins and clipped on to the bit ring. Again this is very neat and easy to undo, but snap billets are not the strongest of fastenings since each time they are clipped and unclipped the spring is made that much weaker. These fastenings are not, therefore, suitable for any sort of strenuous competition.

There are two other forms of rein attachments: buckles and stitching. Buckles can be either square or rounded, neither being better than the other; but the danger is that they are used mostly on cheap bridles and the quality of the metal, particularly the tongue, is usually correspondingly poor. Their other failing is that buckles are inclined to catch on to anything with which they might come into contact. Added to that is the fact that they look untidy, buckling up as they do on the outside of the bridle with the ends poking out. They are, however, easy to undo for cleaning, which the stitched variety are not.

Reins used to be passed through the bit rings and stitched or sewn back on themselves, particularly in the hunting and showing fields, but now this form of attachment is reserved almost exclusively for racing. Sewn reins, again, look very smart and there is very little possibility of the reins coming undone, provided the bridle is properly cared for. Their obvious disadvantage is the fact that the bit cannot be changed without having it cut off thus shortening the reins, and the new bit stitched in its place. Neither can it be taken apart for thorough cleaning.

NOSEBANDS

Cavesson noseband

The simplest form of noseband is the ordinary plain, cavesson, with the two straps either slotted through the noseband and sewn back on themselves or stitched directly on to the noseband. The former method of manufacture is the stronger one and it is to be recommended if a standing martingale is to be used. It also has the advantage of keeping the shape better, the stitched-on ones tending to drop down in front and behind with continual use. The cavesson noseband serves no very useful purpose other than as an attachment for a standing martingale, but it improves the look of the head, particularly a large, long head, and it has become a standard form of 'dress'.

The stitched noseband is a variation on the above, being a much narrower noseband with several rows of stitching along the front. It is used extensively on show bridles and is most suitable for fine, Thoroughbred- or Arab- type heads, but it is not, of course, so strong as the wider plain leather cavesson.

The third variation on the cavesson is the sheepskin-covered noseband. It is used mainly on racehorses, although it was devised in America for use on trotting horses, but is now frequently seen on all types of horses and ponies engaged in diverse activities. The theory behind it is that it restricts the horse's vision, preventing him seeing something out of the corner of his eye, and thus not shying at it; but the vast majority of people buying it today are merely following a rather out-moded fashion. It may help prevent the nose from being rubbed when a standing martingale is used.

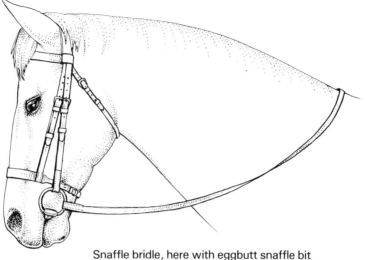

Snaffle bridle, here with eggbutt snaffle bit
and cavesson noseband.

A group of nosebands which do serve a useful purpose, should the horse require one of them, are the 'drop' varieties which include the ordinary drop noseband, the Grackle or figure-of-eight, the Flash and the Kineton. The drop, Grackle and Flash are designed to close the mouth, and are therefore useful for horses who pull and open their mouth or cross their jaws in an effort to evade the bit. They can all be stitched or plain.

Drop noseband

The drop noseband exerts pressure on the nose, causing a lowered head carriage and greater flexion at the poll, and when it is used in conjunction with the snaffle (of which more later), allows greater pressure to be placed on the bars of the mouth than would be the case with a cavesson, the snaffle normally acting purely on the corners of the mouth. By putting his head in the correct position the rider has therefore greater control of the horse. It is, however, important that the drop is correctly fitted and not too low so as to affect the horse's breathing. Approximately 3 in (7 cm), four fingers' width, above the nostrils is about the right place and the strap should be taken outside the bit rings and buckled not over-tightly, so that it lies in the curb groove. As a rough guide, there should be room for one finger between the noseband and the nose. It is important, too, that the noseband is not too narrow, thus enabling the pressure to

be spread more evenly along the nose. The drop noseband is usually fitted with two small metal rings, one on either side of the noseband, which are attached to the headstraps, the rear straps and to the noseband itself; and two short metal prongs are inserted from the ring into the noseband and headstraps to keep the former straight so that it does not drop too far down the nose.

Grackle or figure-of-eight noseband

The Grackle or figure-of-eight noseband serves a similar purpose to the drop but is rather more severe and is ideal for horses who cross their jaws. The nosepiece consists of two straps, the upper one attached to the headstraps, which cross over in front. A small piece of sheepskin or felt is attached to the inside of the cross to prevent rubbing. The two straps are buckled, not too tightly, behind the jaw, the top one above and the bottom one below the bit and there is a leather strap at the rear connecting the two and keeping both in place. It should be adjusted slightly higher than the drop, and is more severe because the pressure on the nose is only over one spot and not right round the nose.

Flash noseband

A standing martingale (*see* Chapter 5) should not be used with either of these nosebands, so if a martingale is required, as well as a drop, and you do not want to use two nosebands together i.e. a cavesson and a drop, then a Flash noseband is often used. This is an ordinary strong cavesson

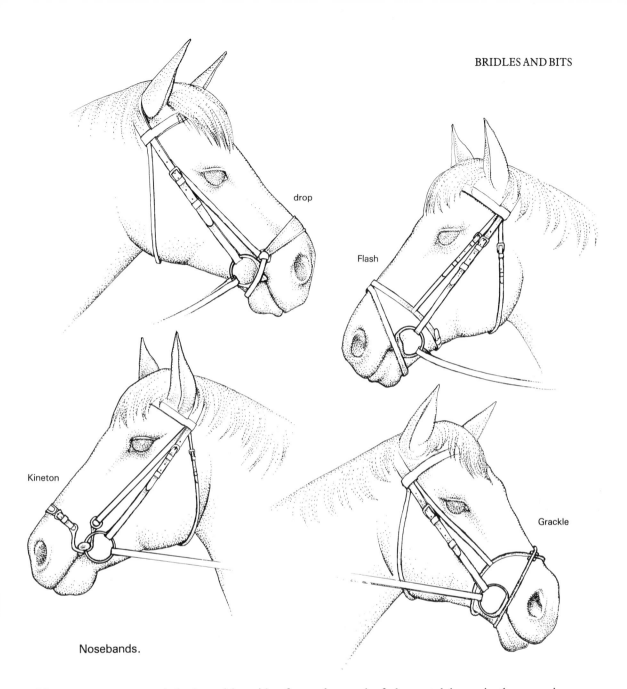

drop

Flash

Kineton

Grackle

Nosebands.

with one or two straps stitched on either side of the front, crossed over and buckled in the curb groove. Again it should be fitted slightly higher than the ordinary drop.

Kineton noseband

The Kineton is reserved for the very strong pulling horse, since it is more severe than any of the foregoing. It consists of the headstraps, which are adjustable on both sides, and are sewn at one end on to two semi-circular metal loops. At the other end of the metal loops is the nosepiece which can be adjusted by means of a buckle fastening at both ends. The nosepiece usually has a strip of metal incorporated into the leather to make it stronger. It is fitted inside and behind the bit rings so that the loop comes into contact with the mouthpiece; the higher the nosepiece is adjusted the stronger is the effect. The principal is that the pressure exerted on the snaffle bit automatically affects the pressure on the nose and the horse's head is automatically lowered in consequence.

FITTING A BRIDLE

Bridles are made in four standard sizes: Small Pony, Pony, Cob and Full Size. These tend to be rather misleading, however, since many ponies have cob-size heads and many cob-size animals have small Thoroughbred-type heads. If you are buying a new bridle without the equine being present the saddler will want to know the type of animal for whom the bridle is required i.e. Thoroughbred, Native pony etc. rather than just that the animal, is, say 13.2hh. A sure way to get the right size is to measure the animal's head from the corner of the mouth on one side, going up the cheek, over the poll and down the cheek on the other side to the corner of the mouth.

We have not yet discussed the different bits that can be used, and before we do so, a word about their size. A jointed bit, such as an eggbutt snaffle, is measured by laying it flat and measuring straight between the inside of each ring where the actual mouthpiece starts. A straight bar bit, such as a Pelham, is again measured between the inside of the rings or cheeks. No allowance in size should be made for bits with ports – they are all measured straight. Bits are usually made in sizes from 4½ in to 5½ in (11.5-14 cm) and at ¼ in (6 mm) variations in between. As a rough guide, and depending again on the type of animal, a 14.2hh-15.0hh animal will probably need a 5 in (12.5 cm) bit.

The horse's mouth can be measured by laying a flat stick (an ice-lolly or popsickle stick for instance) in the horse's mouth, across his tongue, and up against the corners of the lips. The mouthpiece of the bit should just protrude at the corners of the mouth so that the lips are not pinched, and the bit should be fitted so that it just creases the corners of the mouth as though the horse were smiling. If it is adjusted too low it will knock on the horse's teeth; particularly if the animal is a gelding, when it is likely to catch against the tushes (which are situated in front of the molars and behind the incisors) and positively be an encouragement for the horse to get his tongue over the bit. (Mares do not have these teeth.) If it is adjusted too high it will pull at the corners of the lips, causing them to become sore or even cut. The bit is adjusted by raising or lowering the buckles on the cheekpieces.

Bits and their action

All bits fall into one of five groups. These are: snaffle, double bridle or Weymouth, Pelham, gag and bitless bridle. All these groups act on one or more parts of the horse's head in order to control the horse by applying pressure through the bit.

The object of the bit, an extension of the rider's hand, is to regulate and control the energy created. Control comes about by the rider positioning the horse's head in such a place so as to prevent the horse evading the bit by one means or another and so giving maximum control over speed and direction. It must not be expected, however, that any bit is going to achieve this happy state of affairs on its own. The horse must first be schooled to engage his hocks underneath him, thus making the most of the driving force (which comes from behind and not in front of the saddle). Only when he is going freely forward, which is achieved by the rider's active use of his seat and legs, in a supple manner, light in front and with a degree of flexion at the poll, should any attempt be made to put the head in a particular position. If an attempt is made too early in the horse's education to enforce a collected head carriage, stiffness throughout the body will result.

The parts of the head upon which the groups of bit act are as follows: the corners of the mouth, the bars of the mouth, the tongue, the curb groove, the nose, the poll, and the roof of the mouth.

The problem of what bit to use increases as more people go galloping and jumping on young or unschooled horses. In the old days people were willing to spend time getting their horses right before taking them hunting or whatever, or gave them to a 'horseman' to school for them. Today everyone wants quick results and the good, old horsemen are no longer there to school the reprobates. Having taught the horse to go forward, riders, quite reasonably, want to be able to control them sufficiently to do what they want them to with a fair degree of success. Showjumping courses, for instance, are built for

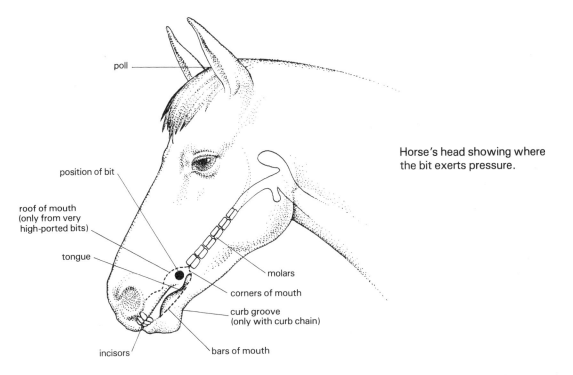

poll

position of bit

roof of mouth
(only from very
high-ported bits)

tongue

incisors

molars

corners of mouth

curb groove
(only with curb chain)

bars of mouth

Horse's head showing where
the bit exerts pressure.

the average horse with the average stride, and 'non-average' horses have to be taught to cope with them as best they can. This frequently leads to problems of restraint, and calls for an ability from the rider to be able to place the horse correctly and to be able to lengthen and shorten strides as required.

Frequently, horses, having got the message to go forward, go too far and too fast for the rider's liking, and a strong, pulling horse who fights the bit is the result. If the horse is fighting the bit, he may, in fact, be fighting the pain in his mouth, so the first essential is to check the mouth for any loose or sharp teeth, sore gums, or tongue, etc, and if these are present call the vet to deal with them.

If there is nothing painful present the horse is probably leaning on the bit and the rider is providing the base against which to lean. In this case the horse must be encouraged to carry his own head instead of you carrying it for him; and a bit, such as the Magenis snaffle, could be used, which has the advantage of a number of moving parts which encourage him to play with the bit rather than lean on it. A pulling horse is usually

made so, however, by a pulling rider on the other end of the reins, and a lighter hand is also indicated as well as a change of bit.

Many horses are just naturally 'onward-going' and although they have good mouths, are just too strong for their riders when out in company or in a competition. For these animals variations of the snaffle (*see* below) can be useful.

THE SNAFFLE

Most equines go perfectly happily in a plain jointed snaffle bit for ordinary hacking, although those with very light mouths may prefer a mullen mouth snaffle. In addition the ordinary snaffle is a mild bit and one that is, therefore, used by novice riders and seen at most riding schools. Although good hands are obviously desirable this only comes with practise; and the novice rider is likely to do less damage to the horse's mouth, while he is learning, with the snaffle than with any other type of bit, whilst still retaining a fair degree of control. The thicker the bit mouthpiece, the milder the bit will be.

The snaffle is the simplest form of bitting and

there are two main types; firstly, the unjointed, half-moon, mullen-mouth snaffle; and secondly, the jointed snaffle. The action in both cases is on the corners of the mouth, the movement being an upward one which raises the head. The mullen-mouth variety is more mild than the jointed snaffle, which produces a nutcracker action in the mouth, whereas the mullen-mouth does not. In the mullen-mouth snaffle a slight degree of pressure is put upon the tongue. Although the snaffle raises the head and acts upon the corners of the mouth, when used with a drop noseband, it has the opposite affect and a downward action is achieved. As a general rule jointed bits are fitted slightly higher in the mouth than the mullen-mouth ones.

Mullen mouth snaffles

These can be made of rubber, nylon, vulcanite or plain metal, of which the rubber is the mildest and the metal the strongest. Rubber bits are in the main used on youngsters or horses with very light mouths, or horses whose mouths have been damaged. Mullen-mouth snaffles (except for the eggbutt) are made with the bit rings loose, i.e. there is a hole at either end of the mouthpiece through which the rings pass, the rings being able to be moved through the hole. Jointed snaffles, however, can be made either with loose rings or with fixed rings. The fixed variety is on the whole preferable, the advantages being that there is less chance of the corners of the lips being pinched and no chance at all of the ring sliding through the mouth in an effort from the horse to evade the bit. The disadvantage is that there is no play at all in the mouthpiece, which is not the case with the loose-ring snaffles.

Jointed snaffles

There are many varieties of jointed snaffles, the commonest ones (in order) being the eggbutt, D-ring, Fulmer, German, Dick Christian, French bradoon, twisted, Scorrier, and Magenis, of which the last three are the most severe.

The **eggbutt snaffle** has a fixed ring and most horses go very happily in it, provided it has a good thick mouthpiece. Too thin a mouthpiece in any bit causes discomfort which in turn leads to resistances. A bit which has gone to the other extreme, in that it is very thick and fat, and therefore mild and comfortable for the horse, is the **German snaffle**; this has gained enormously

in popularity in recent years. It is made with both fixed and loose rings, and so as to reduce its weight the mouthpiece is hollow.

The German mouthpiece can also be found in the **Fulmer snaffle** (or Australian loose-ring cheek snaffle) which was very popular about 10-15 years ago. The Fulmer is used extensively in the training of young horses following their introduction to the bit by way of the keyed mouthing bit (*see* Chapter 6). It is basically a jointed snaffle with cheekpieces, the cheekpieces pressing against one side of the horse's face according to the pressure exerted by the opposite rein. It is, therefore, very useful to help young horses get the initial idea of rein aids. The cheekpieces are slightly curved out at the top, away from the face and leather keepers (bit loops) are used to fasten the cheekpieces of the bit to the cheekpieces of the bridle. The Fulmer snaffle has loose rings set on to metal protrusions which are fixed to the outside of the mouthpiece. It is, therefore, possible for a certain degree of play to take place with this mouthpiece.

A **D-ring snaffle** is very similar to the eggbutt, the only difference being in the shape of the rings; the eggbutt having oval rings and the D-ring, rings in the shape of a letter D.

The **Dick Christian** and the French bradoon are similar in that they both have a link at the join of the two sections of the bit. This link, made of steel, makes the bit less severe than the jointed snaffle, since it lessens the nutcracker action, and the addition of the link lying across the tongue makes the bit more comfortable for the horse. Instead of the two halves of the bit being linked through each other the Dick Christian has a small ring inserted through two holes, one on either side of the centre of the bit, linking the two halves of the bit. There is no play in the joint, but less possibility of the tongue being pinched by the nutcracker action.

The **French bradoon** is milder still, the two sections of the mouthpiece being joined by a small, flat spatular type piece of metal in the centre. In both these bits the bit rings are loose, and both bits can be used successfully on horses who are fussy in their mouths.

The **Dr Bristol**, another similar bit but with the small flat link lying vertically rather than horizontally across the tongue, has a similar

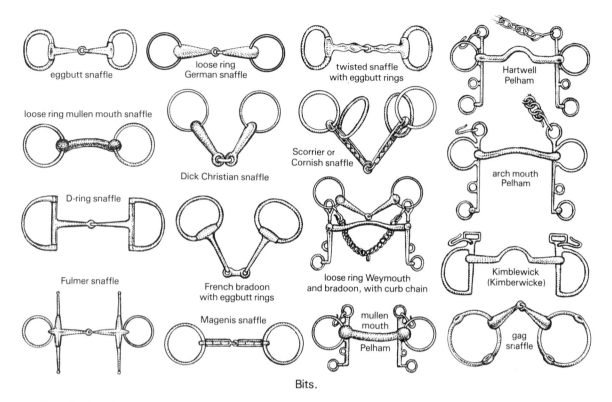

eggbutt snaffle

loose ring German snaffle

twisted snaffle with eggbutt rings

Hartwell Pelham

loose ring mullen mouth snaffle

Scorrier or Cornish snaffle

arch mouth Pelham

Dick Christian snaffle

D-ring snaffle

Fulmer snaffle

French bradoon with eggbutt rings

loose ring Weymouth and bradoon, with curb chain

Kimblewick (Kimberwicke)

Magenis snaffle

mullen mouth Pelham

gag snaffle

Bits.

effect. Both this and the French bradoon reduce the nutcracker action, and avoid the risk of the tongue being pinched by the central joint and of the joint contacting the roof of the mouth.

For the strong, onward-going horse the **twisted snaffle** may be the answer. The twist breaks the smooth surface of the mouthpiece and gives a sharper indication to the horse of what is wanted. It is made with both loose rings and with eggbutt fittings.

The **Scorrier** or **Cornish snaffle** is another stronger bit which can be used with success on strong, pulling horses. It differs from the other snaffles in that it employs two sets of rings, known as Wilson rings. The inside pair of rings are fitted through slots in the mouthpiece itself and are attached to the cheekpieces of the bridle, while the outside pair are for the rein attachments. The mouthpiece itself is either twisted or serrated, and this, combined with the inward, squeezing action on the sides of the jaw when pressure is applied through the reins, often has a restraining effect.

For the powerful horse, one who leans on the bit or crosses his jaw the **Magenis snaffle** may be the answer. It is another loose-ring bit with rollers set across the mouthpiece; their object is to distract the horse from pulling, encourage him to "mouth' the bit and so 'come back' to the rider and give him greater control. It acts principally upon the corners of mouth rather than the bars, thus raising the head.

THE WEYMOUTH OR DOUBLE BRIDLE

If the snaffle is the simplest form of bitting then the Weymouth is the most advanced. It employs two bits: the bradoon (the name given to the snaffle when employed as part of a double bridle) and the curb which is fitted with a curb chain. Because it is the most advanced form of bitting it should only be used on a horse who has reached an equally advanced stage of training and by an educated horseman, but, sorry to say, this is not always the case.

The bradoon which is fitted above the curb in the mouth can be either an eggbutt or loose ring, the eggbutt usually being employed with a fixed cheek curb and the loose ring with a slide cheek.

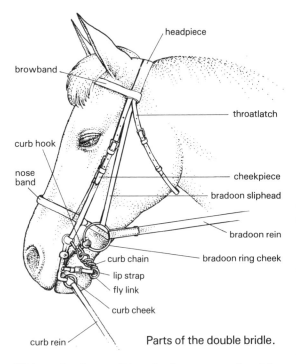

Parts of the double bridle.

Labels on diagram: headpiece, browband, throatlatch, curb hook, nose band, cheekpiece, bradoon sliphead, bradoon rein, curb chain, bradoon ring cheek, lip strap, fly link, curb cheek, curb rein

Either fixed or slide cheeks are used with straight bar bits with a bump in the centre known as a 'port' through which the tongue goes. The port can vary in size and shape, the wider and deeper the port the greater the pressure on the bars of the mouth, and the shallower the port the greater the pressure on the tongue. As the name implies, the fixed cheek has the cheeks of the bit fixed to the mouthpiece leaving no room for play, whereas with the slide cheek the mouthpiece can slide fractionally up and down the cheeks and this is, therefore, slightly more severe in consequence as well as having a less definite action.

A far greater degree of flexion is obtainable with a Weymouth than with any other bitting arrangement, the bradoon acting on the corners of the mouth to raise the head and the curb lying across the bars to lower the head thus retracting the nose. The curb also operates on the poll by means of pressure through the cheekpieces when pressure by the rider's hand is put on the curb rein, and this in turn puts pressure on the curb chain lying in the curb groove behind the lower jaw. The head carriage obtainable is a fairly high

one with the nose carried slightly in front of the vertical and with a degree of flexion at the poll and lower jaw as indicated by the rider's hands on the reins. It is usual in Britain and in the USA for the bradoon rein to be held outside the little finger, and the curb rein to be held between the third and fourth finger which gives emphasis to the action of the snaffle rather than the curb. In European countries, however the opposite is usually the case, and both appear to work equally well.

A curb chain and lip strap should always be used with a curb bit (*see* Chapter 5).

THE PELHAM

The Pelham seeks to combine the advanced results of the double bridle whilst using only one simple mouthpiece and two reins, and, like most compromises, it does not really work. Having said that, however, it must be admitted that there are a number of animals, particularly the cobby types of pony, who seem to go well in it.

The mouthpiece can be either a **mullen mouth** or a straight bar one with a port, called the **Hartwell mouth Pelham,** the former being usually made of vulcanite and the latter of metal. In the more common mullen mouth variety pressure is brought to bear mainly on the tongue, whilst with the ported variety pressure is on the bars. Additionally pressure is on the curb groove, caused by a tightening of the curb chain (which together with a lip strap should always be used) as well as poll pressure; the longer the cheekpieces above the mouthpiece the greater is the pressure, whilst the amount of leverage is directly attributable to the length of the cheekpieces below the mouthpiece. The Pelham's action is somewhat ill-defined, although the snaffle rein generally achieves more pressure on the corners of the mouth (i.e. when the snaffle rein is held outside the little finger) and the curb rein achieves more pressure on the poll and curb groove. Frequently, however, children employ only a single rein, a leather 'rounding' (bit converter) being used to connect the snaffle and curb rings. This, of course, makes the action even more vague, although it is easier for a child to handle only one single rein.

A variation of the straight bar, ported mouthpiece (Hartwell mouth Pelham) is the **arch** mouth Pelham, the mouthpiece of which is, as the name implies, in the shape of an arch. This is useful for a horse with a large tongue, giving it more room than the conventional port and allows a certain amount of pressure to be borne on the bars.

The **Kimblewick** (Kimbelwicke in USA), sometimes called the Spanish Jumping Bit, whilst being a member of the Pelham group, has no cheekpieces as such below the mouthpiece. It has a straight-bar ported mouthpiece and can be made of vulcanite or metal but the rings are similar to those of the D-ring snaffle. It is used with a curb chain. When the hand is lowered the rein slides down the D-cheek bringing downward pressure on the curb groove, poll and bars of the mouth, but to be effective this bit must be used with lowered hands. It is useful for strong horses and ponies, particularly for children jumping strong ponies. Some riders think it most useful for specific activities and for variety, and that used constantly, it can make the horse lean on the bit and the hands.

THE GAG

The gag is basically a snaffle mouthpiece, usually fitted with eggbutt cheeks with holes set in the top and bottom of the rings through which the rounded leather cheekpieces of the bridle are passed before being attached to the reins. Its purpose is to raise the head, the rounded leather sliding through the holes in the bit rings and asking for an immediate upward action. At the same time, however, downward pressure is brought to bear on the poll.

The gag is useful for animals who habitually carry their heads low to the ground, but it should be used with discretion. When employed it should be used with two reins – the one connected by a sewn metal loop to the rounded cheekpieces and an ordinary rein fastened directly on to the bit. In this way the horse can be ridden on the ordinary rein whilst behaving himself and the gag brought into play only when necessary. If the gag is used all the time the horse will become stiff in his neck and back.

THE BITLESS BRIDLE

This is a useful bridle, employing no bit at all, which can be used with success on horses whose

Bitless bridle.

mouths have been injured. It can also be used with success on strong, pulling horses, since when what they were pulling against has been removed – the bit – they often stop pulling. Its action is on the nose with a certain amount of poll and curb groove pressure and since the true bitless bridle, the Blair pattern, employs fairly long cheekpieces, there is a considerable degree of leverage.

It consists of a wide, well-padded noseband, sometimes with a sheepskin covering, with fastenings at the front for adjustment, and long metal cheeks with an additional strip of metal at the bottom, the reins being sewn on to the bottom metal loops. A simple form of bitless bridle can, however, be made from an ordinary strong drop noseband with strategically placed rings for rein attachments.

Whilst it is used with success by some show jumpers *(see page 61)* it is not generally advocated for the more inexperienced rider unless a mouth injury makes other forms of bitting unworkable, when some lessons in its use are essential. It can be an extremely severe form of control when it is incorrectly used.

39

SUMMARY OF DIFFERENT BITS

To summarize this chapter on bitting, the following groups of bit act as indicated dependent upon the horse's stage of training and carriage of the head and neck:

Snaffle – upward action on the corners of the mouth.

Double – basically, an upward action through the bradoon on the corners of the mouth, and downward action through the curb on the bars, curb groove and poll.

Pelham – upward action on corners of the mouth and downward action on the tongue, bars, curb groove and poll.

Gag – upward action on the corners of the mouth and some downward action on the poll.

Bitless – downward action on the nose, poll and curb groove.

The final part of the head with which the bit can come into contact, the roof of the mouth, is only affected if the port of a curb bit is too high and presses on to the roof, or if the roof is unnaturally low, or if, in the case of a jointed snaffle the bit is too big and the joint comes into contact with the roof that way. All these instances are, of course, to be avoided.

There is no hard and fast rule about certain bits being suitable for particular horses with particular problems. Each horse is an individual and must be treated as such – what suits one horse with a problem may not suit a similar horse with the same problem.

However the size and shape of the horse's mouth, particularly the shape of the jaw bones, the size of the tongue, the height of the palate and the thickness of the bars will all need to be taken into account when choosing a bit. For instance, a horse with a low palate will not be suited to a curb with a high port; nor would a fine Thoroughbred type with long, lightly-covered bars be suited to a Pelham, since the curb chain would be likely to rise out of the curb groove and act on the unprotected jawbones. An animal with a small mouth would be unlikely to be comfortable in a double but go better in a Pelham.

For competitive riding when quick and positive action is needed and if the time, inclination or ability for reschooling the animal is not there, a change of bit is often indicated. Horses do tend to get used to certain bits, particularly the stronger ones and every now and again a change is called for, usually to something less strong, if the same response is to be achieved.

Putting on a bridle

The bridle is carried by the headpiece (crown piece), with the reins held there at the buckle. It can be hung over the shoulder and the saddle carried on the same arm, leaving the other free for opening doors or gates.

Unbuckle the noseband and throatlatch, and lipstrap, if used, on near side; unhook curb chain on near side, if used. Hold the headpiece in the left hand, putting reins over horse's neck with the right. With the cheekpieces in your right hand, rest it on the horse's nose, and draw the bridle upwards until the bit is next to the

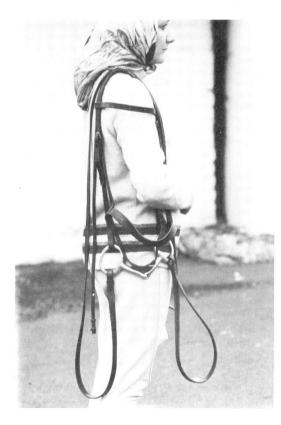

Left: A correct way to carry a bridle, leaving the hands free.

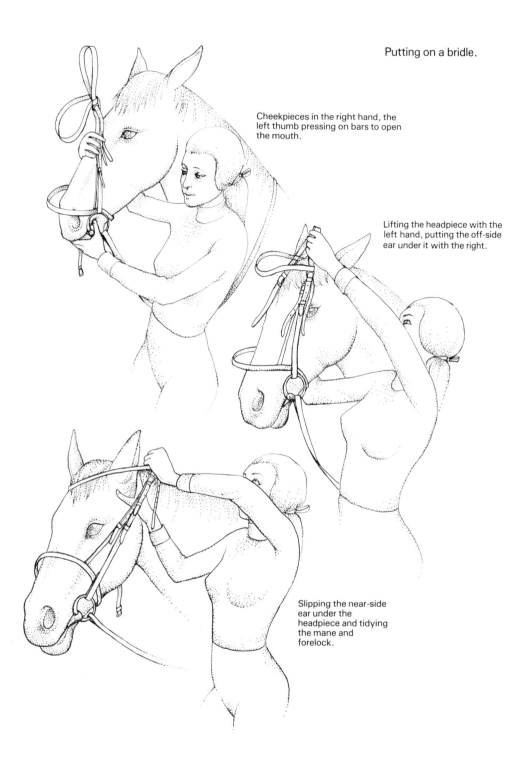

Putting on a bridle.

Cheekpieces in the right hand, the
left thumb pressing on bars to open
the mouth.

Lifting the headpiece with the
left hand, putting the off-side
ear under it with the right.

Slipping the near-side
ear under the
headpiece and tidying
the mane and
forelock.

Putting up a snaffle bridle.

that everything is level and straight, and that the bit(s) are neither pinching nor too low, and do up the noseband. Slip all straps into their keepers. Straighten out the curb chain, if used, so that it lies flat against the chin groove and place it on the near-side hook. Put the strap end of the lip strap through the curb chain's fly link and buckle it loosely on near-side D-ring on bit cheek.

There are also other equally satisfactory methods of putting on a bridle, not described here.

Removing a bridle

Undo throatlatch and noseband, and curb chain and lip strap if used. Take the reins over the head, put your right arm under the horse's neck with your right hand on his nose. Take the headpiece in your left hand, free the ears one at a time and gently ease the bridle off.

Putting up a bridle, and general care

A bridle should be hung on a bridle rack, or a half-moon shaped block of wood, or a saddle soap tin fixed to the wall, so the headpiece keeps its shape. If the bridle is not being used for some time the reins may be hung straight down on a separate peg. Alternatively they may be looped up with the throatlatch which is then buckled. The noseband is then put around the rest of the bridle and the strap end through its keeper.

A bridle should not be left on the ground while the saddle is being put on, but hung on or over something. If a horse is left in a loose box (box stall) tacked-up, he must be tied up fairly short with the headcollar over the bridle and the reins should be tucked under the run-up stirrups. A horse should never be tied up by the reins.

mouth. Put your left thumb into the mouth and press on the bars, the gap between the incisor and molar teeth. Lift the bridle slowly with the right hand slipping the bit(s) past the teeth with the left. Take the headpiece by the left hand, put the right under the neck and put the off-side ear under it, then bring the right hand back and slip the near-side ear under. Place the forelock over the browband and tidy the mane. (About 1 in/ 2.5 cm of mane may be trimmed off where the headpiece lies, if wished, taking care not to remove too much.) Do up the throatlatch. Check

4 Fitting and choosing a saddle

Fitting

The construction of saddles has been dealt with in Chapter 2, so suffice it to say that the tree should, ideally, be built to fit the back of the individual horse for whom it is intended. This, of course, is not always possible for a riding school, for instance, to put into practice, but should be a viable proposition for the ordinary one-or two-horse owner. If one saddle is used on a number of horses it will, in all probability, fit all of them reasonably well, provided they are all of a similar make and shape, but will fit no horse absolutely correctly since it will not have a chance to mould itself to the shape of one individual's back. It may, therefore, cause a sore back in due course, together with a possible hollowing of the back, which in turn, of course, will restrict the animal's movement and, causing general discomfort, affect the horse's concentration and willingness to work.

As already mentioned, saddle trees are made in narrow, medium and wide width fittings and although a medium width will fit most horses it should be ensured that the right width is chosen for the animal concerned. If, for instance, a narrow tree is used on a horse for whom a medium or wide tree should be used it is very likely that the points of the tree will press in to the horse's back. Likewise if a broad tree is used on a horse requiring a narrow or medium tree, the pommel will come down on to the horse's wither, again causing pressure to come to bear on the animal's back.

Pressure and friction are, in fact, the chief causes of sore backs, and if these are to be avoided attention should be paid to certain factors when fitting and buying a new saddle.

Firstly, the saddle must be both high enough and wide enough to clear the backbone and withers. The front arch of the saddle at the pommel should clear the withers by about three fingers' width; this should be tested with the rider sitting in the saddle when the extra weight is brought to bear on the horse's back. The tree must also be wide enough so that the points of the tree do not pinch the horse just below the wither, but not too wide so that the front arch presses on the wither. Any pressure will, of course, inhibit the animal's movement. It is possible for a good saddler to stretch a narrow tree to make it broader, but making a broad tree narrower is never successful.

If the tree fits the back it follows that the panels, provided they are properly made, will follow suit. The panel must bear evenly over the whole length and breadth of the back so that the rider's weight is distributed over as large an area as possible without any pressure being borne by the backbone itself. In order for pressure to be kept well away from the backbone the panel must be kept sufficiently well stuffed. The stuffing must be even throughout the panel because if one side is stuffed more than the other the rider's weight will not be spread evenly, and pressure will be brought to bear on one particular place.

Although stuffing throughout should be plentiful to ensure clearance of the backbone, it should not be over stuffed, as this will make the

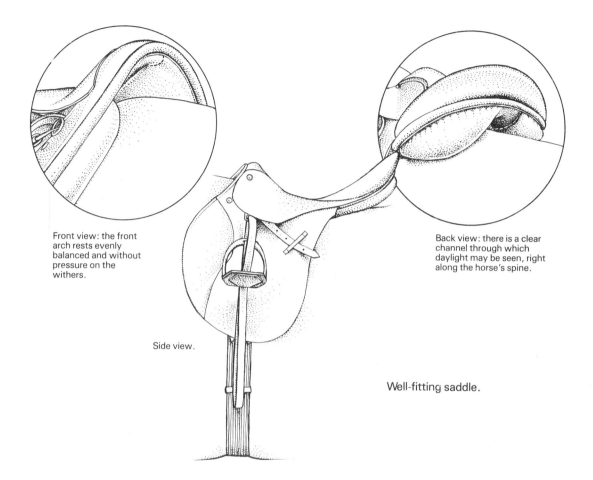

Front view: the front arch rests evenly balanced and without pressure on the withers.

Back view: there is a clear channel through which daylight may be seen, right along the horse's spine.

Side view.

Well-fitting saddle.

saddle rock back and forth over the back and cause friction. A saddle that is evenly stuffed to start with can become uneven by the rider not sitting correctly and placing more weight on one side of the seat than on the other. This is often the case if the rider has his stirrups one hole shorter on one side. It often happens, too, that the horse's back is developed more on one side than the other as a result of the early training having been carried out more on one rein than the other.

The saddle must also fit the horse lengthwise as well as in width, a horse with a long back can wear a slightly longer saddle than a horse with a short back. Saddles are made usually in four lengths: 15 in, 16 in, 16½ in and 17½ in (38 cm, 40.6 cm, 42 cm, and 44.5 cm), 16½ in or 17½ in (42 or 44.5 cm) being suitable for most average horses and riders with average backsides to sit in them. If the saddle is too long it will put the rider's weight over the horse's loins, an area where he is least able to cope with weight. The loins are the weakest part of the horse's anatomy and weight on this area prevents the horse getting his hindlegs under him, thus restricting the free forward movement; in due course it may well damage the kidneys which lie immediately beneath the loins.

It should also be remembered that equine backs, especially those of ponies, change shape according to whether they are living out in the summer on lush grazing, or stabled during the

winter and in hard work. It is inadvisable, therefore, to try to fit a saddle on an over-fat pony as
his shape will change when he comes back in to
work.

It may happen, of course, that a horse ac-
quires a sore back in spite of the saddle fitting
correctly. In this case it is usually because the
animal is unfit and in 'soft' condition; for instance when he has had a long lay-off and is
brought back in to hard work too quickly. The
soreness is caused by the friction of the saddle on
the back and in this instance no saddler can be
expected to alter the saddle to fit. The answer
lies, of course, in prevention rather than cure;
work should be introduced gradually, starting
with short periods of slow work to harden up the
muscles. It is possible, if the unfit horse has to
be worked for longer periods, to harden up the
back by applying surgical spirit to the saddle and
girth area, or, failing that, salt and water will
harden up the skin nearly as well. But prevention is the real answer.

There are two further contributory factors
that may well result in a sore back. The first is
the 'heavy rider' who continually bumps about
and moves around in the saddle, resulting in
friction on the horse's back, as mentioned
earlier. The second can be caused by the rider
grabbing hold of the pommel and particularly
the cantle of the saddle and heaving himself on
to the horse's back. Continual mounting in this
fashion will not only cause friction on the horse's
back but will also, if the saddle is a spring tree
one, cause the springs of the tree to twist, thus
pushing it out of shape; once this has occurred
there is nothing the saddler can do to rectify
matters. Always, when mounting, put the hand
right over the back of the saddle to where the
flap joins the seat – it is just as easy to get up and
no harm will come to the saddle – or, if the
animal is too large to mount comfortably, either
use a mounting block or get a 'leg up'.

PROBLEM FITTINGS
The majority of horses and ponies can be fitted
with a saddle without too much difficulty but
there are some animals whose conformation
makes fitting a saddle a problem. Fat, Thelwell-
type ponies, for instance, who are kept at (on)
grass, are permanently spherical, have no wither

or waistline, and a back like a table-top, will
present a problem in keeping the girth from sliding forward and consequently the saddle also.
The girth should fit into the natural sternum
groove just behind the elbow, but over-fat
ponies lose this groove. In this case, the girth
should be fitted on to the two rear girth straps
and a tubular web girth with a strip of pimple
rubber incorporated into the centre of it will
help to keep the saddle in the correct position.
Failing this a crupper (see Chapter 5) can be used
with complete success. A saddle with a full panel
is more likely to stay in place than a half-panel,
as there will be a greater bearing on the pony's
back.

There is no reason, however, why a waistline
and a wither should not be induced to appear by
turning the pony out with a roller on, provided,
of course, that the pony and roller are checked
regularly. A reasonable shape will be further induced if the roller is passed through a section of
rubber motor-tyre inner tube at both the wither
and sternum areas, since the rubber will help the
pony to sweat off the excess weight. Alternatively a strip of oilskin can be wound round the
roller and used with equal success.

A saddle which slips backwards, which can
happen if the pony has a very flat back, can often
be made to stay in place by having an extra grith
strap fitted in front of the existing ones and
underneath the point of the tree. This is called a
point strap; the girth can then be fastened to this
strap and the first of the existing straps, thus
bringing the girth slightly further forward.

When purchasing a new saddle, the best way
to ensure that it fits both the horse and rider for
whom it is intended is to ask a good saddler to
come out and fit a saddle for you, but failing this
it is possible to measure a horse for a saddle
yourself. A piece of flexible cable (or lead strip
or coathanger wire) should be placed over the
horse's wither at the point where the pommel
fits, and down both sides of the animal's back to
approximately on a line level with his shoulder.
Press the cable well down on the back so that it
matches the shape of the back; without altering
the shape in any way, remove it from the back,
place it on a large piece of paper and draw carefully round it. Another measurement and draw-
ing taken across the back at approximately the

position of the cantle should then be taken, and one more, from pommel to cantle, will give the saddler a good idea of the animal he has to fit. Since the animal may not be exactly the same shape on both sides of his back, remember to mark which side is the near and which the off (the near side is the left side of the horse when sitting on top and the off is the right side). It is as well for the rider to visit the saddler himself so that the saddler can ensure that the saddle is right for the rider too. Many saddlers have a model horse in the shop so that the rider can try sitting in the various types and sizes of saddle to see which he finds most comfortable and suitable for the activity in which he wishes to participate.

Choosing a saddle

Saddles are designed to fulfil certain requirements imposed by particular activities, although the principles are the same for all riding disciplines. As mentioned in Chapter 1, the most important considerations of saddle design are to ensure that the saddle is comfortable for both horse and rider and that the rider's weight is placed over the centre of gravity. If these considerations are fulfilled the horse will be able to perform to the best of his ability and the rider will be assured of maximum security.

It follows that the design of the saddle will alter in accordance with the activity being undertaken, the rider's weight needing to be carried either more or less forward. The two extremes would be the race seat and that adopted for dressage. In the former the weight is over the advancing centre of gravity and in the latter the point of balance is moved slightly to the rear of centre.

Racing aside, there are three main types of saddle corresponding to the activities for which they are best suited i.e. dressage, showjumping and general-purpose or all-purpose, the latter being suitable for cross-country, hunting, long distance riding and ordinary hacking. The difference between the three types is determined by the shape of the tree and the consequent cut of the flaps. In all cases, the tree of the modern saddle has a central dip to the seat, thus putting the rider in the lowest part of the seat, and all have a knee roll, often made of suède, thus giv-

ing support to the rider's thigh just above the knee. Some, in addition, have a thigh roll at the rear to assist in keeping the girth straps from sliding off the panel.

The saddle head or pommel is where the difference begins, as it is to this that the points and stirrup bars are attached.

DRESSAGE SADDLE

Although many dressage saddles are built on a rigid tree, a great number are now also built on a spring tree. Unless it has a cut-back head, the dressage saddle has a straight cut, vertical head which enables the stirrup bars to be positioned fairly far to the rear so that the rider is positioned centrally and in accordance with the movement of the centre of balance to the rear when the horse is in a state of collection, particularly in the advanced movements of *piaffe* and *passage* when the croup is lowered. To conform with this requirement, and to accommodate the longer leg position required, the flaps, following the line of the tree, are almost straight.

A number of dressage saddles, particularly the German ones, have a cut-back head, the idea of this being that it makes the fitting of a saddle on an animal with very high withers easy to accomplish, but a cut-back head does tend to put the rider too far back in the saddle, thus putting more weight over the horse's loins and, in addition, weakens the saddle arch. Saddles with cut-back heads are, however, very popular especially in Europe.

The panel of a dressage saddle should be free from any unnecessary bulk, so that as close a contact as possible can be obtained by the rider. Most dressage saddles, too, are fitted with two instead of three girth straps, which are much longer than normal and extend below the end of the flap. The object again is to reduce any unnecessary bulk in the form of buckles under the flap and to position the rider closer to the horse. A very short belly girth is used in conjunction with this saddle but care must be taken to ensure that it is of the correct length if chafing at the elbow is to be avoided.

Darker coloured saddles tend to be favoured for dressage and Havana and Warwick shades tend to be more popular than the London colour.

Saddles.

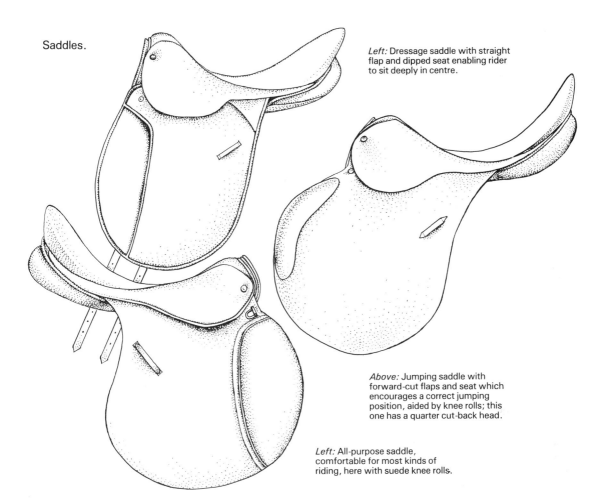

Left: Dressage saddle with straight flap and dipped seat enabling rider to sit deeply in centre.

Above: Jumping saddle with forward-cut flaps and seat which encourages a correct jumping position, aided by knee rolls; this one has a quarter cut-back head.

Left: All-purpose saddle, comfortable for most kinds of riding, here with suede knee rolls.

SHOWJUMPING AND GENERAL-PURPOSE SADDLES

Virtually all jumping and general-purpose saddles are built on a spring tree although a rigid tree can be used. These saddles, too, can have a cut-back head, but the more satisfactory style, and the one which more effectively can assist the positioning of the rider's weight, is that in which the head is sloped and not cut-back. The greater the slope of the head the further forward will the stirrup bars be positioned. A showjumping saddle therefore will have a greater degree of slope than one used for general purposes. The points and the bars, set considerably further forward than is the case with the dressage saddle, result in very much more forward-cut flaps, since the

latter must follow the line of the sloped head.

Federico Caprilli (1868-1908) was the first to put forward the principle of the 'forward system' of riding and many saddles were subsequently designed with forward-cut panels and flaps. The turning point, however, came as a result of a design by a Spanish horseman, Count Ilias Toptani, who, using a spring tree saddle, made the seat deeper and sloped the head further forward than of old.

The sloping head of Toptani's design (which was developed for showjumping) whilst placing the rider in the correct position for jumping, was not quite so suitable for cross-country work and hacking since it placed the rider too far forward. The sloping head was, therefore, modified to

47

form what we know as the general-purpose saddle, the angle of the slope being reduced so that it came somewhere between the dressage saddle and the jumping one. For the general rider, not specializing in dressage or showjumping, the general-purpose saddle will suit most needs.

Again, as in the dressage saddle, the Continental pattern panels have become widely used, and Havana or London colour tend to be more popular shades.

Many modern saddles of all types have a gusset inserted at the rear of the panel which allows for a greater amount of stuffing to be inserted, and makes it easier to ensure that the saddle rests level on the horse's back.

Putting on a saddle
The saddle can be carried either along the forearm with the pommel towards the elbow, or vertically, lining inwards, the cantle under the arm

Right: Putting on a saddle: place gently down and slide back.

and the hand round the pommel. The bridle can be hung over the same shoulder, leaving the other arm free. Stirrups should be run-up and the girth laid over the saddle waist. The girth should be done up on the off side.

Tacking up is normally done from the near side but the horse should get accustomed to it being done from either side. Lift the saddle to forward of the normal position, place it gently down and slide it back. Go to the off side, pull the girth down, and check that the buckle guard and sweat flap are in position; return to the near side, check these here, and put the girth through the martingale loop, if used. Buckle the girth, not tightly. Run your hand under the girth to see that no skin is pinched. With a fat horse, or one with a long coat, it can help to pull each foreleg out in turn, to smooth the skin. Tighten the girth just before you mount.

Removing a saddle
If necessary, allow the horse to cool gradually by loosening the girths on your return and leaving the saddle on a few minutes. Run up the stirrup irons. Undo the girth, and bring the saddle gently on to your left arm, left hand on the pommel and right hand on the cantle. Lay the girth over the saddle waist, inside downwards.

Putting up a saddle, and general care
A saddle should be kept on a bracket on the wall or on a saddle horse. Preferably, the girth and stirrup leathers should hang straight from hooks; or be laid across the saddle. The irons can be hung on pegs.

A saddle should never be dropped, and bumping it should be avoided since the leather will scratch easily, and it is possible to damage the tree. If placed on the ground the saddle should rest on the front arch, and never be laid down flat, since this may also damage the tree. It should not be left where it could be kicked or trodden on. Stirrup irons must always be run up when the horse is not being ridden.

Left: A correct way to carry a saddle, the irons run-up and the girth over the waist.

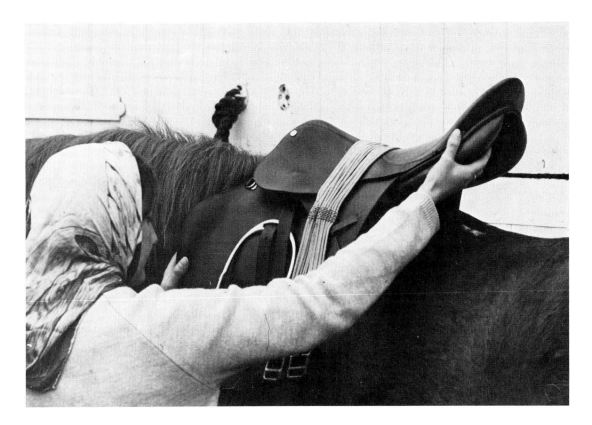

Below: Putting on a saddle: pulling the buckle guard down over the girth buckles.

Below: Tightening the girth before mounting. The end of the stirrup leather is neatly in the loop on the saddle flap.

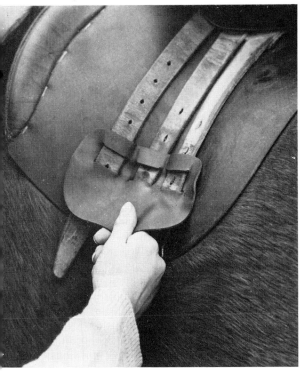

Above: It can help to prevent the girth pinching to pull each foreleg out in turn, especially with a long-coated or fat horse.

Left: The correct way to stand a saddle on the ground, resting on the pommel and preferably leaning up on a vertical surface.

5 Saddle and bridle accessories

Saddle accessories

Stirrup leathers

These are most frequently made from strong cowhide, the best being oak bark tanned, but are also made of either buffalo hide or rawhide, i.e. specially tanned cowhide. Both these last types of leather and are very strong; buffalo is reddish in colour. Rawhide and cowhide stirrup leathers are made with the grain side of the leather, which is the strongest side, facing inwards, so that any movement of the stirrup iron on the leather is taken by the side most able to take the friction, thus ensuring that the leather will not wear thin. Buffalo hide leathers are, however, designed with the usual flesh side facing inwards since both sides are of equal strength and virtually unbreakable. Cowhide does not stretch to the same extent as either rawhide or buffalo hide but neither is it as durable. The buckles are usually made of stainless steel, or the metal mixtures Kangaroo or Eglantine, the leather passing over the bottom piece of the buckle and being sewn back on itself.

All stirrup leathers stretch with use, and since few riders ride with their weight equally placed on both irons it is a good idea to change the leathers over from time to time, so that the stretch becomes equal on both sides. Some leathers are punched with holes fairly close together, known as 'half holes' and it can be very helpful to use these when new leathers are in the process of stretching. The most usual stirrup leather widths are $\frac{7}{8}$ in, 1 in and $1\frac{1}{8}$ in (2.2, 2.5 and 2.9 cm) and they do, of course, come in different lengths, children requiring shorter leathers than adults.

For small people who ride large horses, and therefore have difficulty in mounting, an extending stirrup leather might well be the answer. The leather, which is attached to the nearside stirrup bar in place of the ordinary leather, has, fitted on to the bottom piece of the buckle, a small metal hook. Also fitted to the bottom of the buckle is a strong piece of tubular web, about 8-10 in (20-25 cm) long, and this is attached to another metal fastening into which is incorporated a slot. The web folds back on itself and the slot fastens back on to the hook. The leather is attached to this metal fastening, the leather passing over the bottom piece of metal and being stitched back on itself in the usual way. The idea of this extending leather is that the leathers can both be adjusted to the required length, the nearside one can then be unslotted from the hook thus making it longer and easier for mounting. When the rider is in the saddle the leather can easily be slotted over the hook again so that it is at its original shorter length. Not long ago these were in common usage but today they are not so frequently seen although they are still obtainable from a good saddler.

STIRRUP IRONS

The most satisfactory stirrup irons are made of stainless steel or one of the mixtures such as Kangaroo or Eglantine. They can also be made of nickel but these are unsatisfactory since they are easily bent and broken.

There are three main types of stirrup iron: the

ordinary plain iron; the Kournakoff and the child's safety iron known as a Peacock iron.

Standard plain iron

The standard plain iron is in most general use and should be as large, within reason, as possible without being so large that the foot can slip through; and good and heavy, so that the foot can come out easily in the event of a fall. These irons are perfectly satisfactory for all equestrian activities.

Kournakoff iron

The Kournakoff iron, named after the Russian cavalry officer who invented it, has the sides of the iron sloped, the tread sloped upwards and the slot of the iron through which the leather passes set just off centre and to the inside. The idea of the Kournakoff is that it ensures that the rider's toe is kept up and the heel down; and by having the slot placed 'off true' the bottom of the foot is carried higher on the outside than the inside. This has the effect of pressing the knee and thigh into the saddle and thus, since this position gives greater security, particularly when a shorter length of leather is used, the Kourna-

koff is particularly suitable for showjumping. If used, however, care must be taken to ensure that the irons are on the correct sides, otherwise considerable problems will be incurred. It is not suitable for showing or dressage when the restriction imposed on the leg position is not desirable. It is sometimes called the offset iron.

Peacock iron

The Peacock iron is still frequently used by small children but has dubious advantages. The tread, one side, the inside, and the top with the slot for the leather are made of metal and are as in an ordinary plain iron, but the ouside has a thick rubber band stretching from a hook at the top of the iron to another at the base near the tread. A small leather loop fastens the rubber band to the hook at the bottom. It was designed to ensure that if the child fell off the rubber band would come undone and the child's foot would be free, but the disadvantage is that the rubber ring is liable to come undone even when the child does not fall off. In addition, the tread tends to become bent downwards through the child constantly putting pressure on the iron

Stirrup irons.

Peacock child's safety iron

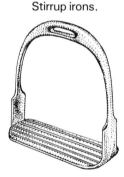

Standard plain iron,
here with rubber tread (pad)

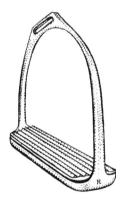

Kournakoff, or offset iron

Three-fold girth

Atherstone girth

Balding girth

when mounting, which results in the foot being forced into the wrong position, the outside of the foot being carried lower than the inside.

Rubber stirrup treads (stirrup pads)

A number of people now use a grooved rubber tread inserted in the ordinary iron. This slots through the middle of the tread of the iron covering the whole tread and assists in keeping the rider's foot in the correct position on the ball of the foot. It also prevents the rider's foot from slipping out of the iron as might happen if the rider was wearing leathersoled boots and the tread of the iron had worn smooth. Treads keep the feet slightly warmer in winter.

GIRTHS

Almost certainly the best girths, but also the most expensive, are made of leather, either buffalo hide, rawhide or cowhide, or in the case of the three-fold girth, a very soft leather; there are three common types: the three-fold, the Balding and the Atherstone.

All three have two buckles at each end, made of Eglantine, Kangaroo or stainless steel, through which the leather passes before being sewn back on itself. The best buckles have a groove at the top for the tongue to fit into, and this prevents any likelihood of the tongue slipping through the buckle. These buckles fasten at each end on to the girth straps underneath the flap of the saddle, the purpose of the girth being to keep the saddle in place. Leather girths must be kept clean and supple if they are to wear well and not to rub the horse, since by virtue of their position on the horse they receive a great deal of sweat which dries out the leather and makes it hard very quickly.

Three-fold girths

The three-fold girth is, as its name implies, made from one piece of leather which has been folded over twice to form three layers on top of each other. The girth is used with the folded edge at the front so there can be no danger of the horse being pinched behind the elbow. For extra strength the girth is usually reinforced with two small pieces of leather on both sides of all four buckles. In order to keep the girth supple it is advisable to keep a strip of absorbent material soaked in neatsfoot oil inserted into the inner fold of the girth.

Atherstone girths

The Atherstone also has four small pieces of leather to reinforce the buckle attachments, and in addition has a fairly narrow strip of leather running straight down the centre of the girth. The advantage of this girth is that it is shaped, so that it is narrower in the centre part where it is positioned behind the elbows, and wider at each end for the standard attachment to the girth straps. This means that there is no danger of chafing the horse behind the elbow and making him sore, possibly resulting in girth galls, as could happen when a horse in soft condition is being brought into work.

Balding girths

The Balding girth, too, is shaped so that it is narrower in the centre portion. In this instance it is made narrower by the leather being divided into three equal sized strips about a quarter of the way down from the buckle, the strips being plaited once each side before coming into one thick central piece of leather.

Lampwick girths

The material which vies with leather as being most suitable for girths is lampwick, a soft, tubular white fabric which is very strong and considerably cheaper than leather. It is reinforced with leather at the buckle ends.

Nylon girths

Nylon cord girths in various colours are popular, cheap and fairly satisfactory except that the binding near the buckle ends tends to come undone; and the buckles, in order to accommodate all the nylon cords, tend to be fairly large, thus causing a lump under the saddle flap, which is uncomfortable for the rider.

Web girths

Finally web material can be used for girths although it is not in such common usage as of old. However the white tubular web girth with pimple rubber in the centre is a very useful one to use on plump ponies to keep the saddle in place. This comprises two narrow strips of web to which the buckle is attached at each end and reinforced with leather. In the centre the webbing becomes wider and the pimple rubber is fastened on the inside, thus giving a grip to the pony's sternum groove.

The old-fashioned web girths comprised single strips of web, the better ones being of wool web, about 3 in (7 cm) wide with a buckle at each end. They were sold in pairs and were usually navy blue or grey in colour, and whilst being fairly cheap to buy had to have the sweat washed off frequently if they were not to chafe. Whilst not so frequently seen today they can still be obtained from good saddlers. They are likely to break suddenly when in use.

Lampwick, nylon and web girths should all be washed regularly if the sweat is not to make them hard and cause chafing. Care should, however, be taken to ensure that the leather reinforcements and buckles do not get too wet, and grease or oil should be well rubbed in to both.

Buckle guards or girth safes

Whatever type of girth is used, however, it is advisable to use a pair of buckle guards or girth safes. These are small pieces of leather or synthetic material with three slots in them which can be slid through the girth straps on the panel of the saddle, one on each side, before the girth is attached. The girth is then buckled on to the straps underneath them. They are inexpensive and prevent the buckles from wearing a hole in the saddle flaps. Make sure they are over the buckles after tightening the girth.

CRUPPERS

A crupper is a useful piece of equipment to use on an over-fat pony whose saddle persists in sliding forwards. It is a long leather strap with holes punched at one end and a buckle in the centre which passes through the D-ring on the saddle (i.e. a metal ring which can be fixed to the bottom of the cantle) and fastens back on to the centre buckle. The other end of the strap is divided in two with a buckle at each end on to which is fastened the dock piece. This is a U-shaped piece of leather, very well stuffed in the centre which tapers at the ends into which holes have been pinched. The U-shaped piece goes under the horse's dock and the ends of the straps fasten on to the buckles of the long strip of leather which lies down the centre of the horse's backbone. It should be adjusted just tight enough to keep the dock piece in place without being uncomfortable for the horse and must be kept well oiled if it is not to cause chafing. When

so adjusted it keeps the saddle in place very satisfactorily.

A crupper is also used, attached to a roller, when lungeing and breaking a horse (*see* Chapter 6).

BREASTPLATES

A useful item which can be used on horses whose saddles slide backwards is a breastplate. As well as in the specialist fields of racing and polo, when a somewhat different pattern is always used, breastplates are frequently used on hunters, especially those who are ridden in very hilly country when the saddle is most likely to slip.

Breastplates consist of several strips of leather fastened by means of buckles. One piece of leather with a loop at the end through which the girth is passed goes from the girth, between the forelegs to the centre of the breast where it is sewn on to a metal ring. This ring should be backed by a piece of sheepskin or leather if it is not to rub the horse. From here two divided straps pass one either side of the neck where they buckle on to two further metal rings. These two rings are joined by a strong leather strap which is sewn on to the rings and passes over the wither. Two further short straps are passed through these rings and on to the D-rings of the saddle before being buckled back on themselves. (Metal D-rings can, again, be attached to the front arch of the saddle by any good saddler.) Adjustments for fitting are by means of the buckles, usually on all the straps except the wide front one crossing the wither. If either a running or standing martingale is to be used with a breastplate, a simplified version eliminating the girth attachment can be attached to the central breast ring by means of a buckle.

A much simpler form of breastplate (*see* Chapter 8) is used to assist in keeping rugs in position.

NUMNAHS (SADDLE PADS), WITHER PADS (POMMEL PADS) AND SADDLE CLOTHS

Numnahs are basically saddle-shaped pads which are attached to the panel of the saddle by buckles, tape or nylon fastenings or loops, and which lie underneath the saddle with the wool side lying on to the back. Although they appear to be very popular additions to the normal tack, and are frequently seen on children's ponies, their purpose in many cases is purely decorative, since provided the saddle fits the back well they are unnecessary. If the saddle does not fit well the long term answer is to get it restuffed, not to use padding underneath.

They also tend to cause the back to overheat, especially with more finely-bred horses, thus increasing the likelihood of sore backs. In addition, since modern saddles are designed to have minimum bulk under the flaps (so that the rider can be positioned as close to the horse as possible, thus allowing the use of finer aids) it would seem somewhat contrary to put a thick numnah underneath the saddle, and thus an extra thickness between the leg and the horse.

Nevertheless, there are some horses who suffer from a 'cold back' and for these a numnah can be helpful and much more comfortable. The term 'cold back' is frequently used of a horse who may possibly have some disorder of the kidneys or loins. A cold back results in the horse's back sinking down when he is saddled up.

Numnahs are traditionally made of sheepskin, some of them linen backed, or more generally today of nylon simulated sheepskin. If they are used, care should be taken to keep them clean and free from sweat which causes the wool to become hard and knobbly and so can cause pressure points on the back; so frequent brushing and washing (with soap, not detergent which will irritate the skin) is indicated.

More common today are the cotton-covered foam numnahs, which are much easier to keep clean and do not create the problem of lumps of sweaty wool forming, which is experienced with the sheepskin variety.

With both varieties, however, care must be taken when putting them on to ensure that the numnah is pushed right up into the channel of the saddle, leaving a clear space over the wither and along the length of the backbone to avoid creating friction.

Wither pads (pommel pads) too, are not necessary so long as the saddle fits, and if it comes down on the wither a pad should only be used as a temporary measure until restuffing can take place. Traditionally again wither pads are oval shapes of knitted or woven wool, usually navy blue or grey in colour, but sheepskin pads are also seen.

Plain or checked linen saddle cloths are sometimes seen on children's ponies, and are again unnecessary and positively detrimental. They are not padded in any way and are used purely as ornament. The danger is that the tapes which are sewn onto the saddle cloth and tied underneath the flap of the saddle, apart from causing an uncomfortable lump under the rider's thigh, are rarely sewn in the right place, which means that the cloth creases under the saddle and is liable to cause a sore back. If one is used, again make sure that it is pushed right up into the channel or a sore wither is likely to result.

Bridle accessories

BIT ACCESSORIES
Curb chains

A curb chain should always be used with a double bridle or Pelham bit, since when rein pressure is applied on the curb bit, a backward and downward pressure is applied on the lower jaw through the curb chain as it tightens. It is fitted on to the hook of the curb or Pelham bit on one side, and then passed either through the largest ring of the bit and through the equivalent ring on the other side of the bit fixing on to the curb hook again; or directly on to the hooks on both sides without passing through the bit rings. There are varying opinions as to which is the correct way but the former is certainly more satisfactory when a Pelham is used if any sort of pressure is to be applied; otherwise the curb chain can fall away when the curb rein is operated, the chain rising above the curb groove. Whichever method is employed, however, care must be taken to ensure that the chain lies flat in the curb groove and is not twisted before hooking on to the opposite curb hook. Adjustments can be made to the length of the curb chain by hooking up the chain a couple of links on either side, but make sure that the small ring (fly link) at the bottom of the chain stays central.

Curb chains can be made of either metal or leather, the metal ones being either double or single linked and can be of varying widths. The double linked, wider variety is preferable as it is less sharp than the single linked chain, is easier to make lie flat, and the pressure is distributed over as wide an area as possible. Leather curb chains are kinder still, provided the leather is kept soft so as not to cause chafing. They have three metal links at each end joined by a wide strip of stitched leather with a central metal loop stitched into the middle. It is possible, too, to obtain elastic curb chains which again have three metal links at each end, the whole being joined by a strip of thick elastic, and these too are perfectly satisfactory.

If a metal curb chain does cause chafing a rubber curb chain guard can be obtained which slots through the chain, the wide piece of rubber lying next to the horse leaving the gap in the centre on the outside.

Lip straps

A lip strap, too, should always be used with a curb or Pelham bit and curb chain as this prevents the chain from rising out of the curb groove. The lip strap consists of two small strips of leather, either flat or rounded, the larger strip having a small loop at one end and holes punched at the other, and the shorter piece having a small buckle at one end and a small loop at the other. They are attached to the two small loops on the curb or Pelham bit, one on either side, the longer strap being fastened to the nearside loop by being passed through the loop on the bit and then back on itself and through the leather loop on the lip strap. It then passes through the ring on the curb chain and buckles on to the shorter strap which is attached to the bit in similar fashion on the off side.

Roundings (bit converters)

For small children who cannot manage to cope with two reins, but whose ponies wear a Pelham, roundings, otherwise known as joiners or couplings, are often used. They do solve the two rein problem but for all other practical purposes they nullify any positive action of the bit. Roundings are rounded pieces of leather with a buckle at each end which buckle through the bit rings, the buckles being fastened on the inside, and to which the single rein is attached.

Bit guards

For a horse who goes well in a snaffle or Pelham but whose lips have become sore at the corners, it is possible to alleviate this soreness by the use of a pair of bit guards. The better ones are made of rubber which can easily be pulled over the bit rings and lie between the rings and the mouthpiece. They can also be made of leather, and these are again circular, but with an opening down one side through which the bit is passed before laces fasten the guard in position. Leather ones do, however, tend to become stiff if not regularly oiled and the laces themselves can cause chafing. If the lips become sore, check that there are no sharp protrusions on the bit and that it is not wearing thin, as this is the most likely cause of soreness.

Neckstraps

A neckstrap is a simple leather strap which fastens round the horse's neck with a buckle. It may be a stirrup leather or the neckstrap part of a martingale. To prevent it slipping forward it can be attached to the front D-rings of the saddle with two small leather straps with buckles, like a breastplate. The neckstrap provides something for the rider to grab hold of in moments of need, thus saving the horse a jab in the mouth from the reins being grabbed. It is useful when teaching beginners, particularly jumping; for early riding on a young horse; and for riding in hilly country.

REMEDIES FOR EVASIVE BEHAVIOUR

A number of horses, usually those whose initial training is not all that it might have been, develop unfortunate means of evading the movement and action required. They do this in a number of ways, for instance, shying, bolting, getting above or behind the bit, putting the tongue over the bit and so on. Given the time, knowledge and facilities, retraining can often cure these misdemeanours; but for those without these requirements there are various pieces of tack that can at least minimize and in some cases cure the faults.

Brush prickers (bit burrs)

Some horses tend to be one-sided in the mouth or stiff in the back, favouring one side, and for them a circular piece of leather with a hole in the centre, containing groups of short bristles can be helpful. It is fitted over the bit rings in a similar way to bit guards, the bristly side facing inwards towards the mouth. Known as a brush pricker, it is fitted to whichever side the horse favours in an effort to cause him sufficient discomfort for him to move away from it and go straight.

There are then quite a number of horses and ponies who have the annoying habit of getting their tongue over the bit. This habit usually starts because the bit, particularly if it is a jointed one, has been fitted too low in the mouth in the early stages of training, thus giving the horse something to play with. With the tongue over the bit the rider's control is lessened and the action of the bit nullified.

To prevent him getting his tongue over the bit a mullen-mouth bit should be used, as this is not so easy to get his tongue over as a jointed bit.

Tongue ports

If he still gets his tongue over, a rubber tongue port can be attached to the mullen mouthpiece. This is a thick piece of rubber with a small tongue-shaped flap of rubber on one side which lies backwards along the tongue. On the other side is a rubber loop through which the flap is passed, the central rubber piece being curved so that it lies round the mouthpiece of the bit. The flap is pulled tight and straightened so that it lies flat along the tongue.

Tongue grids

If the habit persists there are two further devices which may work. The first is a tongue grid, which is a piece of metal shaped like a rounded 'W', which fits into the horse's mouth, being adjusted above the bit. The tongue grid is suspended in the mouth, the bottom of the 'W' resting on the corners of the lips, its object being to prevent the horse retracting his tongue which he has to do in order to get his tongue over the bit. The top of the 'W' has fixed metal loops. These are attached, either by buckles or by stitching, to an extra strap, known as a slip head (the same type as that which secures the bradoon of a double bridle).

Tongue-over-bit devices

The second device, known simply as a tongue-over-bit device, may also prove successful, comprising as it does two circular leather rings, similar to bit guards, one of which is fitted either side of a mullen mouthpiece, the discs being laced together in the usual way. To these rings are attached two leather straps, one with holes punched in it, and the other with a buckle fastening, which buckles over the horse's nose. In the centre is stitched a small leather strap,

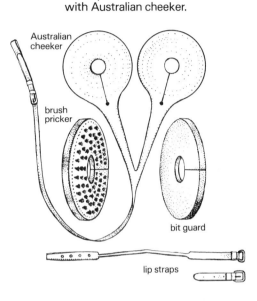

Brush pricker (bit burr) with Australian cheeker.

Australian cheeker

brush pricker

bit guard

lip straps

again with holes punched in one end and a buckle on the other; this passes over the centre of the cavesson noseband and buckles back on itself. This contraption has the added advantage of bringing pressure to bear upon the nose.

In the USA a tongue tie may be used. Before any of these devices are used, however, the animal's mouth and particularly his tongue should be checked to see that it is not sore or being pinched by the bit in any way, since one of likely reasons for him getting his tongue over the bit is that he is trying to ease any pain.

There are then those horses who insist on pulling and running away. If a change of bit does not work (often a change to a milder rather than a stronger bit will be effective), there are two pieces of tack which exert a mental rather than a physical means of restraint.

Australian Cheekers

The first is the Australian Cheeker, which is a strip of rubber similar to an upside-down 'Y'. At the top of the single rubber strip the rubber is reinforced with leather which has holes punched in it and a buckle, and this passes over the centre of the headpiece and buckles back on itself. The central rubber strip lies straight down the nose before dividing into two circular discs similar to bit guards, one slotting through each side of the mouthpiece.

Nose nets

The other device which has met with success is the nose net. This is a small net, similar to a tiny haynet, made of cord or nylon with four leather straps attached, two in front and two behind. The leather straps fasten on to the cavesson noseband, fairly tightly, so that it just touches the muzzle. It inflicts no pain at all but tends to make the horse draw back away from it rather than rush into it.

Both the Australian Cheeker and the nose net can be obtained from good quality saddlers; but if the nose net is not in stock it can often be obtained from farm stockists. It is basically a calf net, put on calves to stop them suckling.

Blinkers

Horses who spook or shy repeatedly may be deterred from so doing by wearing blinkers. The simplest pattern is a silk or synthetic hood with holes for the ears and three buckles fastening under the chin. It is put on over the bridle and is very simple to put on and off.

MARTINGALES

The object of all martingales is to prevent the horse's head being raised and carried to such a high degree that the horse evades the bit, thereby minimizing the rider's control. There are two types of martingale which are frequently seen, the standing and the running, the former being attached to the cavesson noseband and the latter to the reins. Both have a leather neckstrap, which is a thin strip of leather with holes at one end and a buckle at the other, it being fastened round the horse's neck fairly loosely to keep the martingale in place, there being a small loop in the centre through which the wider strap of the martingale passes. Both, too, have a wider strip of leather with a loop at one end which passes through the horse's forelegs, the loop being passed through the girth. Except for the Irish, martingales should have a small red rubber stop where the neckstrap joins the wide strap (which goes from girth to reins or noseband). This keeps any slack in front of the neckstrap instead of behind, where the horse could catch his leg in it.

Standing martingale

The standing martingale exerts pressure on the nose to keep the head down, the other end of the strap attached to the girth being attached by a small loop to the underside (backstay) of the cavesson noseband. There is a buckle fastening on the strap lying between the forelegs which allows the martingale to be tightened or loosened depending on the length required. If it is adjusted too short there is a danger of it restricting the movement of the head and neck. A tight standing martingale, whilst giving the rider greater control, should not therefore be used for jumping where the horse needs the freedom of his neck and head. For ordinary riding it should be adjusted so that it forms a straight line from girth to noseband when the head is carried in the correct position. It should never be used with a drop noseband as the pressure would affect the horse's breathing.

Running martingale

The running martingale brings the head down by exerting pressure on the horse's mouth, the action of the bit, through the downward pull on the reins, being upon the bars of the mouth. The neckstrap and girth attachments are the same as for the standing martingale but after passing through the forelegs the strap divides in two at the end of each strap where there are metal rings sewn on, one rein passing through each ring. This can be a severe aid if it is adjusted so as to form an angle between the horse's mouth and the rider's hand, but, correctly adjusted so that the rings of the martingale come in a straight line across from the withers it is a useful cure for head-raisers.

Rubber or leather rein stops should always be used with a running martingale. These are small, oval loops which have central slots through which the reins, one through each, are passed. They are then slid down the reins to about 8-10 (20-25 cm) from the bit, and prevent the rings of the martingale sliding foward and getting caught in the billet fastening, or even worse, hooked over a tooth.

If a running martingale is used in conjunction with a double bridle, (which should only be done by the experienced rider) the martingale

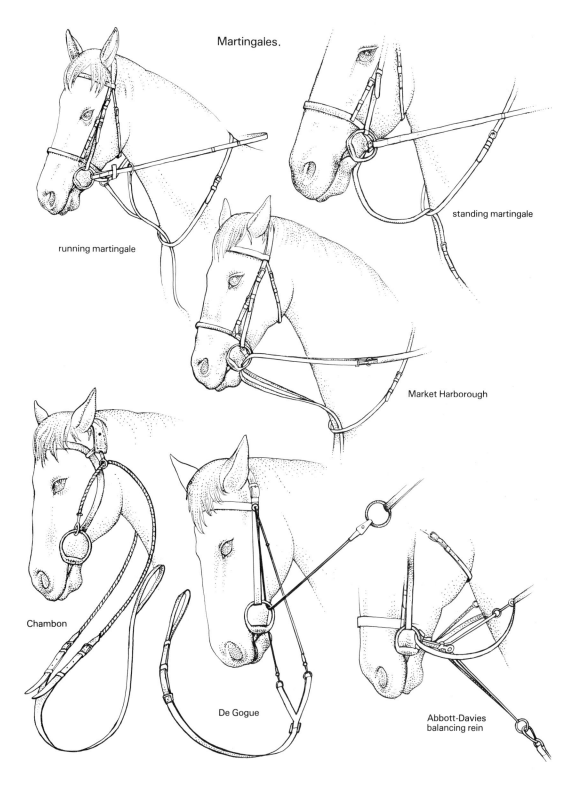

Martingales.

running martingale

standing martingale

Market Harborough

Chambon

De Gogue

Abbott-Davies
balancing rein

should be fixed on to the curb rein, which lowers the head, and not the bradoon rein, which raises the head.

Irish martingale

The Irish martingale is not a martingale at all but a short strip of leather with a metal ring at each end one of which is passed through each rein underneath the head. The object is to stop the reins coming over the horse's head in the event of a fall. This device is usually reserved for racing.

Market Harborough

The other martingale which is sometimes seen on headstrong horses is the Market Harborough. This has the usual neckstrap and girth fittings, but where these join at the centre of the chest, there is a ring to which two pieces of strong leather, sometimes rawhide, are attached by means of a spring hook. These pass up through the bit rings, and buckle, or fasten by another spring hook, on to the rein at one of the four metal D-rings sewn on to the rein itself.

As with the running martingale, pressure is brought to bear on the bars of the mouth, but this only happens when the horse throws his head up. When carried in the normal position the Market Harborough is slack and only comes into play when the horse dictates it. Since, unlike the standing martingale there is no restriction of the head and neck, the Market Harborough is particularly useful on pulling horses in the jumping ring.

Apart from the Irish, which may simply be hung on a peg, these three martingales are best kept on similar brackets to those used for bridles.

In addition to the above there are three other martingales which are used purely as schooling aids to supple the neck and back, so inducing the former to be correctly positioned and the latter to activate the quarters, increasing the engagement of the hocks and counteracting any tendency towards a hollowing of the back.

Chambon

The first of these to be considered is the Chambon, which brings pressure to bear on the poll in order to bring about a lowering of the head. It consists of the ordinary girth attachment which divides in two at the chest, ending in two short straps with buckles at the end. On to this are fastened two leather straps to which two lengths of strong cord are sewn, one length being attached to each bit ring by a spring clip, after passing through a loop which is attached to either side of a padded poll strap. This is kept in place by two small leather loops which are attached to the headpiece of the bridle.

The Chambon can be tightened or loosened, according to the stage of training, at the buckle fastenings at the chest, initially being fastened loosely. The tension is not increased until the head and neck are well lowered and the neck outstretched, thus resulting in a rounding of the back. This device should only be used for short periods at a time, probably no longer than 20 minutes at one session if the horse is not to become stiff and sore; initially, at any rate, schooling should be carried out at a walk.

All work using the Chambon should be carried out either on the lunge or loose in the schooling area, not ridden.

De Gogue

Since the horse cannot be ridden in the Chambon, the De Gogue was devised as an extension to the Chambon and as a device which could be used in ridden work. Pressure is again exerted on the poll as well as on the corners of the mouth. It consists of the main girth strap which divides in two at the chest ending in two metal loops. On to these are attached by means of two snap hooks, one on each side, two pieces of rounded leather which go one either side of the head and attach through two loops to a strong piece of leather which goes over the poll. The leather then continues in a straight line down the sides of the cheeks and through the bit rings and back where it is attached by means of a stud fastening to a metal ring to which the ordinary rein is attached. The whole is used over an ordinary snaffle bridle.

Both the Chambon and De Gogue are fairly advanced schooling aids which should not be used by the inexperienced, but for those who know what they are doing, both are valuable schooling aids which induce the horse to lower his head, flex at the poll and achieve a suppleness throughout the body.

Abbot-Davies Balancing Rein

In recent years the Abbot-Davies Balancing

Rein has come into being, its purpose to 'develop rapidly the muscles in a horse, in order to maintain correct balance, and give maximum performance. Whatever your individual schooling objective, this patent rein will act as an accelerator, doing in a week what would normally take months of work'.

The 'kit', for it comprises no less than 11 different pieces, can be used in three different positions, one principally for lungeing and the other two for increasingly rapid results. Great care should be taken not to work a horse in it for more than short periods of time, as the makers claim that 'in all three positions a horse is beginning to work muscles that have been lazy in the past. Therefore after the first day's use of any of these positions the horse may be a little stiff'.

The kit comes complete with an explanatory booklet so suffice it to say that it can be fitted attached from mouth to girth, from mouth to the tail with a rope or fixed from the mouth to behind the ears with a rubber connection.

In the first position it is not dissimilar to the De Gogue in its effect, the martingale strap being attached to the girth, but at the chest it has a metal snap hook with round strips of leather attached which run over a metal pulley attached by clips to the bit and back to D-rings on the rein. The makers recommend that the second position should be used once to start with, i.e. with no girth strap but with the rope attaching the mouth to the tail, before using the first position.

Whilst the makers make great claims for this rein, it should be stressed that whilst it may well achieve quick results, schooling in it should only be carried out for very short periods of time and by educated and capable riders.

Running martingale used by Irish showjumper Eddie Macken. The horse also wears a bitless bridle, with long metal cheeks and a sheepskin-covered noseband (*see page* 39). Note the loose rein.

6 Specialist equipment

Breaking tackle

When breaking-in a young horse the first items of equipment needed are a lungeing cavesson and lunge rein.

LUNGEING CAVESSON

The cavesson is made of strong leather, and consists of a wide slip head type strap which goes over the poll, buckling on the near side, on to which is sewn, through metal rings at either side, a wide noseband which buckles at the rear. The noseband is reinforced with a metal plate, is hinged at either side and has three protruding metal rings which swivel, one at the centre and one on either side. Where the cheekpieces join the noseband two further metal rings are attached, one on either side for the initial attachment of side reins. A throatlatch or jowl strap is sewn on to the off side of the slip head and buckles on to the near side. Unlike the throatlatch of a bridle, this one should be fastened fairly tightly, as its purpose is to prevent the cheekstraps of the cavesson from sliding round and coming into contact with the horse's eye.

Although not usually sold with the cavesson, a browband is a very useful addition; but because the fitting of the normal fixed type might be difficult to achieve with a young, fractious horse, there is a useful type with an ordinary loop at one end which is slipped through the headpiece in the usual way, with a stud fastening at the other end which can be passed across his forehead and done up when the cavesson is on the horse.

The noseband must be well padded if it is not to rub the horse, and should be adjusted fairly tightly to prevent it from sliding across the nose. In addition to the above rings, it is useful to have fixed to the noseband two extra metal rings, one on either side, just below the cheekstraps, on to which the bit can be attached a little later in the training. The cavesson is not usually sold with these rings attached.

Recently strong nylon cavessons have appeared on the market, particularly pony-sized ones and these are, of course, very much cheaper than the leather variety. Cavessons come in three sizes, pony, cob and horse size.

LUNGE REIN

The lunge rein is made of white or coloured tubular web or 1 in/2.5 cm flat web stitched back on itself at one end to form a loop; at the other end it is stitched to a short piece of leather with a swivel snaphook attachment for fastening to the ring on the noseband. The better ones have a swivel attachment between the leather and the webbing so that the rein does not twist round on itself. Lunge reins should be lightweight and vary in length from about 18 ft to 35 ft (5.5-10.7 m), the longer the better, since, initially at any rate, the young horse should be put on large circles so that his action is not restricted.

Recently nylon lunge reins have been produced to complement the nylon cavessons. These are fairly satisfactory; but when using the nylon variety it is advisable to wear gloves, since if the nylon rein is pulled through the fingers a painful rope burn may result.

Horse equipped for lungeing using side-reins, in lungeing cavesson,
roller, brushing and over-reach boots.

Lungeing is used in the initial stages of the horse's education when it helps to supple and balance the horse and gets him to be obedient to the voice. It is also a useful way to exercise a horse when it is impossible to ride him, and also to let him get the kick out of his heels if he is over-fresh before riding him. It is also a useful way for an adult to exercise a small pony.

LUNGE WHIP
A lunge whip is also necessary, not to hit the horse with but to keep him going forward and to prevent him coming in on the circle. It is usually made of nylon over fibreglass and has a long thong fitted to the end. It should be light and well balanced.

BOOTS FOR LUNGEING
No young horse should be lunged without boots to protect the legs from injury through knocking one leg against the other. Polo boots are possibly the best type to use, these being made of either leather or Kersey cloth with a shaped padded leather reinforcement over the fetlock and tendon area. They are fastened by means of four or

five leather straps and buckles and fit over the horse's cannon bone, giving extra protection to the tendons. However, the straps are an awful fiddle and there are a lot of boots now on the market which are made of foam-lined plastic with Velcro (quick-release) fastenings which are just as good, are quick and easy to put on and off and easy to keep clean. The sound made by Velcro being unfastened may upset a young horse so care should be taken when they are first used.

FIRST BITS
When the horse has become used to going round on the lunge the time will be right to get him accustomed to wearing a bit. The most common mouthing bits are the straight bar and the jointed snaffle bits, both of which are fitted with 'keys', the object of the keys being that the horse plays with them and so keeps his mouth wet. Both bits have loose rings, the straight bar one having a small flat piece of metal in the centre which has three small pieces of metal, the 'keys', hanging from it. The jointed variety has a circular ring of metal in the centre of the mouthpiece and from this hangs the same key arrangement.

Mouthing bits.

Straight bar snaffle mouthing, or
breaking, bit with keys, or players.

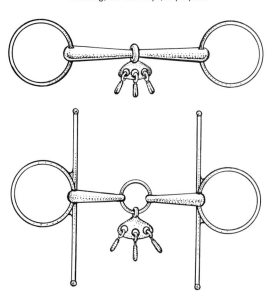

Jointed ball-cheek snaffle mouthing,
or breaking, bit with keys, or players.

The advantage of the straight bar bit is that it makes it more difficult for the horse to get his tongue over the bit, a habit that must be avoided especially at this early stage of training. It is important that the bit is the correct size and is fitted correctly, not too low in the mouth as this again will encourage him to get his tongue over it.

The bit can be fitted to the two metal rings on the cavesson mentioned earlier by two small straps, bit straps, which are buckled up on the outside. If there are no such rings on the cavesson it will be necessary for the horse to wear a plain bridle, without a noseband (which would get in the way of the cavesson) and without reins, underneath the cavesson, with the mouthing bit attached in the usual way to the cheekstraps. After the initial mouthing, (or, before, if it is found that the horse retracts his head and gets behind the bit) a rubber or vulcanite mullen-mouth snaffle is the most sensible bit to use.

LUNGE ROLLER (BODY ROLLER AND SURCINGLE IN USA)

Having become accustomed to being lunged from the cavesson with the bit in his mouth, the horse should be introduced to the roller in preparation for the saddle, and later side reins which will indicate to the horse the initial correct positioning of his head. The best type of roller is in two parts for greater ease of adjustment, and it is made of strong leather with well-stuffed pads which lie either side of the spine. At the bottom of the pads on the outside two strong leather straps with holes punched in them are attached, one on either side. In the centre of the roller and at the back of it should be stitched a metal ring, to which a crupper (*see* Chapter 5) can be attached in due course. At the front of the roller should be stitched two or preferably three metal rings the same distance apart on each side, one near the bottom of the roller, the other about halfway up and the last near to the top, to which the side reins are attached when the time is right.

The other half of the roller consists of a stout leather bellyband, which should be kept supple to avoid chafing the horse. At either end are stitched two buckles for attachment to the other half of the roller. For preference the bellyband should be slightly cut away in the centre at the front, so that there is no danger of it rubbing the horse behind the elbow if the roller slides forward. Other rollers are made in one piece with buckle adjustments on one side only.

CRUPPER

There is a difference of opinion as to whether a crupper should be fitted at this stage, or not until side reins are fitted. One argument is that the crupper prevents the roller sliding forward and also encourages the horse to use his loins to balance himself; whilst others maintain that its use encourages the horse to hollow his back, the opposite of what is wanted.

SIDE REINS

When the horse is going well in this tackle, side reins can be introduced to suggest, not impose, a head carriage. Plain side reins consist of two leather straps or, in the USA, usually nylon webbing straps. One has a swivel spring clip at one end and holes punched at the other; and the other strap has a buckle at one end and another spring clip at the other. The clip is attached initially to the metal ring at the side of the cavesson and later to the bit rings. The straps are adjusted for length by the buckle fastening in the centre. The other end is clipped on to one of the rings on the roller, starting with the bottom ring and gradually working up when the horse advances in his training. A crupper can be fitted at this stage to the metal ring on the back of the roller and going under the dock in the normal way.

There are other side reins available which have elastic or rubber inserts in either side, the theory being that these have more 'give' in them and avoid a dead pull; but an equally valid theory is that they encourage the horse to tuck his head in and get behind the bit. Whichever type is used, however, they should be very light, have plenty of holes for adjustment and be adjusted equally on either side.

The object of side reins is to encourage the horse to reach for the bit, at the same time rounding his back and engaging his hindlegs under him. This will, in due course, when the muscles of his neck and back have been stretched and suppled, result in a raised head carriage, since the hocks will become further engaged thus lightening the forehand. The side reins should therefore be adjusted loosely to start with and lengthened until the horse is stretching and dropping his head and neck. Not until the back and neck muscles have been stretched and tensed and the horse raises his head naturally should the side reins be shortened, their purpose then being to steady the head carriage and perhaps improve it.

After this initial breaking, when the young horse is ready to be ridden on, a modern well-fitting general-purpose saddle should be used and a plain snaffle bridle with either a thick jointed German snaffle or a Fulmer snaffle.

LONG REINS

Long reins are exactly what the name implies – long reins of leather with a buckle or clip fastening at one end for attachment to the bit or cavesson. They are also available in webbing, which is cheaper.

Long reining is out of the province of the vast majority of ordinary riders and trainers, but in skilled hands it encourages the horse in free forward movement. There are four separate schools of long reining: the Danish; Classical (as employed at the Spanish Riding School); French; and British, each employing different methods and different equipment.

The Danish method, where the reins are used from the cavesson through terrets on the top of a roller and passed over the horse's back, can be used on the horse either on straight lines or on the circle and can be used to teach all movements including high school movements; as can the Classical method, when the reins are carried on either side of the back, and straight from the bit. The French method involves the rein going from the bit through terrets at the top of a collar, and down through rings at the side of the roller, before being carried one on either side of the horse; it is used to encourage an almost vertical head carriage. The British method takes the reins from the bit through the rings halfway down the roller, and the horse can be driven either on the circle or straight lines, the trainer walking immediately behind the horse. When on the circle, the outside rein comes round the horse's body on a line just above his hocks.

Competitions and activities

DRESSAGE

A dressage saddle, as discussed in Chapter 4, will be required. For novice and preliminary tests a jointed or straight bar snaffle bridle must be used. Either a snaffle or a double may be used in medium and elementary tests, but for the more advanced tests a double bridle is required. No martingales or other accessories are permitted, but a drop noseband can be used with a snaffle bridle instead of an ordinary cavesson.

SHOWJUMPING

A forward-cut jumping saddle with knee rolls (*see* Chapter 4) will be necessary. In the USA the 'close-contact' jumping saddle is often used; this has no knee rolls. A plain leather bridle should be worn, with either a snaffle, Weymouth or Pelham, or in extreme cases a gag, bit attached, depending on how the horse goes and what he is most comfortable in. Martingales may be worn, although they should not be adjusted so tightly that the horse cannot stretch his head and neck as he will need to do over a fence. Drop nosebands may be worn; but martingales should not be attached to drop nosebands.

Most jumpers wear bandages and/or boots of some sort to prevent injury from striking into themselves or overreaching (*see* Chapter 8).

EVENTING

Eventing or horse trials consists of three separate phases: dressage, cross-country and showjumping, the dressage being the first phase followed in novice events by showjumping and lastly cross-country, but the latter two phases are reversed in advanced competitions.

For novice competitions, a general-purpose saddle will probably suffice for the dressage phase, but in open or advanced competition a dressage saddle will be required. For the cross-country and jumping phases a general-purpose saddle will suffice in all but advanced classes, when a more forward cut jumping saddle is desirable for the final phase.

As a precaution against the saddle slipping it is a good idea to fit a breastplate for the cross-country phase; and a surcingle (overgirth) made of webbing and fastened over the saddle is an extra safeguard against a girth strap breaking or coming undone.

A snaffle bridle will be necessary in all but advanced events, when a double bridle will be required.

As in showjumping, most eventers wear some form of protective bandage and boot to protect them against knocks and bangs. In advanced competitions a minimum weight limit is laid down and horses have to wear a weight cloth (weight pad) containing lead underneath the saddle. Alternatively, so as to avoid carrying too much 'dead weight' riders may carry some built into their clothing – boot heels for instance.

In all disciplines a general-purpose saddle and snaffle bridle are sufficient for exercising.

LONG DISTANCE RIDING

Whatever tack is used for long distance riding, it must fit well; and be light, supple and comfortable for both horse and rider, since both are going to have to use it for a considerable length of time over long distances. Care must be taken to ensure that the weight is spread evenly over the horse's back; but what saddle is used is a matter for the individual's preference, so long as the essential requirement of comfort is fulfilled.

In Australia and America, this form of riding has been in existence for much longer than in Britain and the distances covered are considerably greater, often lasting over several days covering rocky terrain; military saddles are sometimes used. These distribute the weight along the full length of the saddle and at the same time air is allowed to pass freely along the spine. In Britain ordinary general-purpose saddles are usually used, frequently with a numnah underneath.

During distance training it must be remembered that the horse's back will change shape as he gets fitter, so care must be taken to see that the saddle fits well at all stages of his training programme. It is useful for the horse to wear a breastplate if hilly areas are to be covered, but it is advisable to keep all equipment down to a minimum.

Any type of bridle may be worn, the lighter the better but snaffles are most widely seen. Bitless bridles are also quite popular.

HUNTING

An ordinary general-purpose saddle and plain leather bridle with either a snaffle or double bridle is all that is required for hunting. Rubber reins are a good idea as they do not slip so easily when wet, as is a breastplate to keep the saddle in place in hilly terrain. Martingales are also quite permissible and frequently seen, as are boots and bandages.

GYMKHANAS

An ordinary general-purpose saddle and preferably a plain snaffle bridle is all that is required for gymkhana games, although there is no ruling on other equipment. However gymkhana ponies do tend, in the rush of excitement, to get pulled about rather and too strong a bit, which could be used unintentionally to jab the pony in the mouth, should be avoided. Bandages and boots are frequently worn, as are martingales.

SIDE-SADDLE RIDING

This elegant style of riding is now reviving in popularity; at bigger shows there may be several classes for it: lady's hack ridden side-saddle, a riding class and a class for ponies. It can be an attractive part of a carousel or entertainment.

All side-saddles are designed for the legs to be on the near side, where there are two projections, or pommels. The right leg rests over the higher one, the left leg under and against the lower one, the left foot in the single stirrup iron. On the off side of the saddle is a balance strap, a wide leather strap going diagonally from the side of the saddle seat and buckling on to the girth, which helps to keep the saddle level. The seat is often made of doeskin. A side-saddle must be a very good fit.

Showing equipment in Britain

IN-HAND CLASSES

Foals should be shown in a smart leather or nylon slip or headcollar, with a long leather or webbing lead rein; unbroken youngstock in a narrow, stitched, brass-mounted headcollar, perhaps with a white leather browband, and leather or webbing lead.

Alternatively a narrow stitched 'slip head' can be used: a very narrow noseband without a rear strap, with brass buckles on each side to which the headpiece is attached. To the two brass rings on either side of the noseband is attached a 'coupling', either a brass chain with clip hooks or a leather strap again with brass buckles. Both couplings have a central ring to which is attached the lead rein. This looks good on Arabs and other youngstock with small, pretty heads. For a youngster who is broken, if more control is required, a mullen mouth vulcanite snaffle can be used attached to the headcollar or slip head by means of bit straps again with brass buckles, and in this case the coupling is attached to the bit rings. Broken youngsters may also wear a narrow show bridle with lead rein.

The lead rein is a shorter edition of the lunge rein, about 8 ft (2.4 m) in length, but with a brass buckle fastening and no swivel between the web and the leather. More recently narrow leather

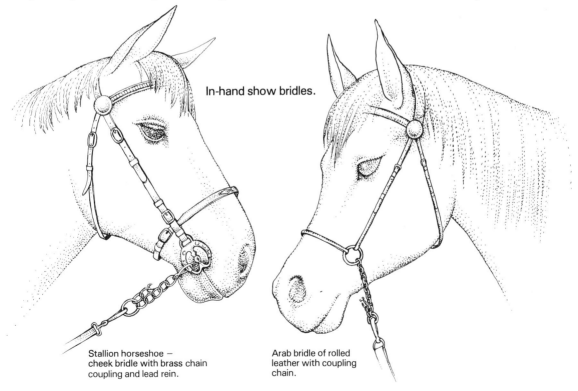

In-hand show bridles.

Stallion horseshoe –
cheek bridle with brass chain
coupling and lead rein.

Arab bridle of rolled
leather with coupling
chain.

lead reins have come into vogue and these are just as good.

Geldings and mares in pony classes wear a show headcollar with or without a bit, and a white or leather lead rein. In-hand hunters are shown either in a double bridle, or in a snaffle, with a lead rein. Arabs may wear special show bridles which accentuate their features.

Brood mares are normally shown in a plain snaffle or double bridle with the reins used as a lead, small native mares usually in a snaffle. Pony youngstock may wear coloured browbands. They can equally be shown in a headcollar with or without a bit. Welsh section C and D mares are sometimes shown in white hemp halters.

Stallions aged three or over wear an in-hand stallion bridle, which is a bridle with brass buckles instead of billets. In addition it usually has a brass disc at either side of the browband. The bit should be a straight bar 'stallion bit' which has small horseshoe shaped brass cheeks. Attached to this should be a brass chain coupling with a leather or web lead rein of sufficient length for the handler to be able to hang on to should the stallion stand up on end, as they are prone to do. Frequently, too, stallions are shown with smart leather rollers with side reins attached from the rings on the roller to the bit rings and they wear a crupper. The side reins are a help if the stallion is unruly.

RIDDEN CLASSES

In all ridden show classes a straight-cut saddle should be used, the idea being that the horse's front and shoulder is shown to maximum advantage, and it gives the illusion of the horse having more in front of the saddle than perhaps he has. Show saddles for hacks and Arabs frequently have doeskin seats and flaps. Stirrup leathers should have half holes punched in them, thus allowing for plenty of adjustment for judge's lengths of leg, and care should be taken to ensure that the stirrup irons are large enough for the judge's foot. Except for small show ponies, when white web girths are permissible, girths should be made of leather. Numnahs or saddlecloths should not be worn.

Except in novice classes, when snaffle bits should be worn, a double bridle will be required for all exhibits. Bridles should be neat, clean leather ones, the width being suitable for the individual's head. Heavyweight hunters and cobs with large heads, for instance, will not look right in a narrow bridle. Equally a fine Thoroughbred head will be swamped by a wide one. Plain leather browbands should be worn on all exhibits except show ponies and hacks, when a coloured velvet-covered one may be worn. For small fine Thoroughbred or Arab-type heads, be they pony, hack or Arab, a narrow or rolled leather bridle with a rolled or stitched leather noseband looks smart. Hunters and cobs look best in a plain bridle. Drop nosebands should not, of course, be worn, neither should martingales, nor leg bandages nor boots.

In pony classes, tack varies according to the class. For the leading rein, novice and child's first pony classes a snaffle bridle is used, the leading rein of white webbing or leather being fastened to the noseband. A felt saddle with a tree may be used for a very small child, otherwise a leather one. For other pony classes a straight-cut show saddle with a narrow elasticated girth is used. The bridle is usually a narrow leather, fancy stitched show bridle with double bits and reins. Snaffle bridles are also permitted. Coloured browbands are allowed, but numnahs, martingales, leg bandages and boots are forbidden.

It is always wise to check carefully any rulings on tack in the show schedules.

Show equipment in the USA

American horse shows reflect the wide variety of riding styles and different breeds that have developed in this vast country. Basically the riding styles can be divided into three types; the hunt seat which originated in England; the stock seat developed by the American cowboy; and the saddle seat which developed on the plantations in the Old South. Although all the American breeds can be shown in all three seats, it is usually the Thoroughbred that is seen in hunt seat and jumping classes, the Quarter Horse which excels in stock seat classes, and the Tennessee

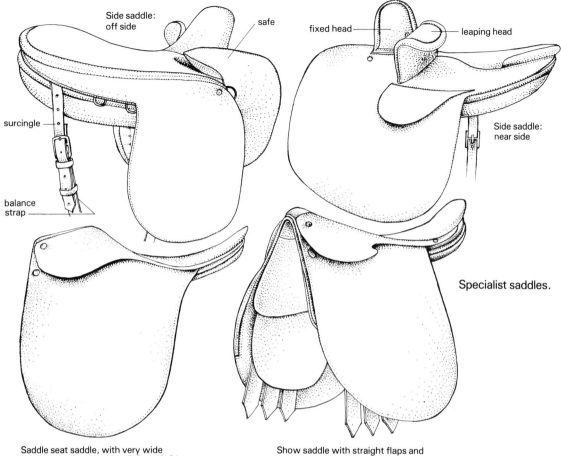

Side saddle: off side

safe

fixed head

leaping head

surcingle

balance strap

Side saddle: near side

Specialist saddles.

Saddle seat saddle, with very wide flaps (extending to within 5-8 cm/2-3 in of the cantle), the flat seat encouraging the rider to sit well back.

Show saddle with straight flaps and recessed stirrup bars to reduce bulk at the knee, here with vertical, or straight-cut, head.

Walking Horse and American Saddlebred that come into their own in saddle seat classes.

All the various breed shows have both in-hand 'halter' classes and performance classes.

HUNT SEAT CLASSES

The hunt seat classes include those for hunters, jumping and horsemanship classes, and all hunters have to jump in the ring, marks being awarded for their style of jumping, with the exception of the hunter under saddle class. The judge never rides the exhibits. Hunter classes are then divided into green hunters, for those in their first or second year of showing; pony hunters for those under 14.2hh; junior hunters to be ridden by those under 18 years; adult/amateur hunters for those ridden by non-

professional exhibitors over 18 years; working hunters in which the horse's conformation is not taken into account; and conformation hunters in which the conformation plays the major part.

Jumping classes are similar to those in Britain with divisions similar to hunter classes.

For hunt seat equitation classes, a snaffle, Pelham or full double bridle is used, with a cavesson noseband. A martingale is optional for the jumping phase only. An English type forward-cut saddle is used. For hunter and jumper classes, again, a snaffle, Pelham or double bridle, with a cavesson noseband, is used, and an English hunting saddle. The girth should be leather, threefold leather or web, without elastic. Rubber reins, stirrup pads (treads) and saddle pads (numnahs) are not permitted.

Horse in decorated Western tack, including a breastplate, for a stock seat show class.

STOCK SEAT CLASSES

Stock seat events include the Western classes with Western tack being used, the most popular classes being those for equitation, pleasure classes and those for trail horses.

For stock seat equitation classes the saddle will be Western, and must be comfortable for horse and rider. It can have a slick or swelled fork and a high or a low cantle. A *lariat* or *reata* (lassoo) must be attached to the fork. A Western bridle and bit is used; if a curb chain is permitted it must be at least ½ in (1.3 cm) wide and lie flat against the jaw. Reins may be split or closed, but if they are closed, hobbles should be carried. (For other Western classes, *see* page 77.)

HALTER OR IN-HAND CLASSES

For youngstock a fine leather or nylon halter should be worn, with a bit, if appropriate, according to age and training; these should suit the breed and particular class. Arabs are shown in finely-designed leather show halters or show bridles, which display their heads to best advantage. Western youngstock entries are shown in substantial leather show halters and bridles with ornamentation of silver conchas and scalloped plates. Youngstock who will mature to hunt seat types are shown in an English style leather show halter or show bridle of finely stitched leather with chrome or brass mountings.

Stallions are shown in a stallion bridle and bit, with a surcingle, side reins and crupper.

Other halter entries may be shown in full (double) riding bridles and led with the reins, or according to the breed or class.

It is wise to check any rulings on tack in the prize list of a show, or the American Horse Shows Association Rule Book.

Many horses competing in America are under the direction of professional trainers, who operate stables where they train horses and riders for the show ring. These trainers usually specialize in one of the three seats, often specializing still further, handling, for instance, juniors only and acting primarily as an instructor, while others will concentrate purely on the horses without teaching any riders. The trainers are usually responsible for a number of horses under their personal supervision both at home and at shows.

SADDLE SEAT CLASSES

Saddle seat classes include equitation classes for juniors in which the style of riding only is taken into account. Five-gaited horses are expected to perform at the walk, trot and canter as well as the two artificial gaits, the slow gait and the rack; while the three-gaited horses perform the flat-footed walk, the running-walk and the canter.

Horses are shown in a full double bridle, and a cut-back saddle which is designed to enhance and encourage the natural action of the animated show horse. It is straight-flapped and allows maximum freedom of the shoulder and high head carriage.

7 Western and stock saddlery

Development of the Western saddle

Western riding equipment is based on that of the 16th Century Spanish Conquistadores and it was subsequently used, little changed, by the Mexican *vaqueros*, North American's first cattle ranchers, who operated in the Southern States. Since the saddles (a mixture of Moorish and European styles) had been designed to assist the horseman in battle, the emphasis was based very much on security with a very high pommel and cantle, a deep seat and a long stirrup leather. The tree was made of wood and was covered in rawhide.

When the whole concept of cattle ranching changed, as it did following the US Civil War, cattle were then herded for very considerable distances in the Southern States to the rail head which served the Northern States; and the cowboy's saddle, too, changed in design, for use over greater distances.

Comfort was now a pre-requisite for both horse and rider since both had to cover long distances in all weathers. To add to the horse's comfort, a thick blanket was folded several times and placed under the saddle since the saddle itself was not padded. Although the saddle was heavy, often weighing as much as 50 lb (22.7 kg), it was designed so that the weight was spread evenly over as wide an area as possible thus ensuring that there were no pressure points. There were extremely wide sweat flaps, called *sudaderos*. The saddle skirt, which corresponds to the flap on an English sadde, was made longer and wider.

'Fenders' (or *rosaderos*) were introduced. These are strong wide pieces of leather, attached under the seat jockey and correspond to stirrup leathers on the earlier Western and English saddles. They serve a dual purpose, in that being wide, they covered the rider's legs, thus affording protection from the fierce sun and heavy rain of the desert plains, as well as from mud and sweat from the horse's sides. They also gave protection against the thorny cacti with which the desert abounds. In addition the fenders, like the stirrup leathers, held the stirrup. Because the fender is stiff, the stirrup does not move when the cowboy puts his foot in to the stirrup to mount, thus he is able to mount quickly and easily – a necessity on occasions.

Again with an eye to comfort, the stirrups were made of varying widths of willow wood frequently covered with rawhide, a more sensible material to use under desert conditions than metal, which quickly gets hot under the sun and very cold in the winter weather. Foot and stirrup coverings, known as *tapaderos* were frequently used for warmth and protection. Made of strong leather and attached to the stirrup, the *tapaderos* form a box round the stirrup into which the cowboy puts his feet.

One of the most important aspects of the cowboy's work, however, was roping the steers by means of a lassoo or lariat or *reata*. To take the strain of the roped steer the cowboy secured the rope to the front of the saddle. Although the Mexican saddle had a high pommel, it did not

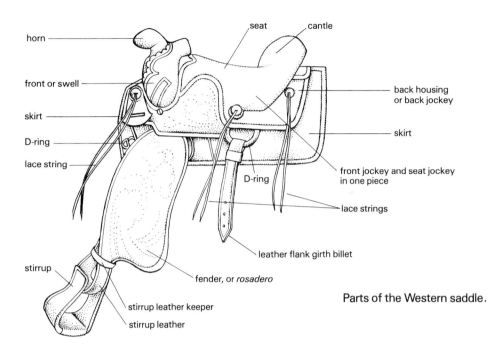

horn

front or swell

skirt

D-ring

lace string

stirrup

seat

cantle

back housing
or back jockey

skirt

front jockey and seat jockey
in one piece

lace strings

D-ring

leather flank girth billet

fender, or *rosadero*

stirrup leather keeper

stirrup leather

Parts of the Western saddle.

have a horn on to which the lassoo could be fastened so this had to be added. But in order for this to be used satisfactorily two further modifications had to be made. Firstly the front arch of the saddle had to be reinforced with steel and widened so that the arch cleared the withers. This meant that a 'front' or 'swell' was created at the front arch leading up to the horn, which provided further security for the rider.

It was found, however, that the strain of the roped steer on the horn of the saddle pulled the saddle forward and upwards, often damaging both the horse's shoulder and the tree of the saddle. To overcome this, the single cinch (the equivalent of the English girth), which was fastened slightly further forward than the normal position (just behind the horse's elbows), in the Mexican saddles, was strengthened by the addition of a further cinch which fastened round the horse's ribs just behind the rider's leg, the second modification made. The front cinch was fastened loosely and only tightened up when the pressure on the horn started to pull the saddle upwards. A saddle fitted with one cinch is known as having 'single rigging', whereas one

employing two cinches has 'double rigging'. The second cinch is also referred to as the 'bucking cinch', as it keeps the back of the saddle from rising if the horse bucks.

Although leather straps are employed to attach the cinch to the rigging rings which are attached to the saddle, the front cinch is made of horsechair, cord or mohair, the ends being woven on to large rings. The flank cinch is, however, made of leather with a buckle at each end, and these are attached by straps in turn to another set of rigs known as 'rigging rings' at the rear of the saddle. To prevent the loosely-fastened flank cinch from sliding too far back and possibly causing galling, a further strap connects the two cinches underneath the horse's belly. One further addition to the Mexican saddle was a set of strings which were attached to either side of the skirts of the saddle and to the pommel, to which the cowboy fixed his possessions.

There were, however, regional differences in the basic Western saddle, developed due to the variations in terrain in which the cowboys worked. In California, for instance, the roping was performed in a slightly different way, as the terrain was easier to work on; no flank cinch was employed as the cowboy played out the lassoo when roping, thus bringing the steer to a gradual, as opposed to a sudden, stop. This meant that the saddle did not need to bear such a strain. In the more mountainous areas a breastplate made of leather or cord was often employed. It was fastened to the D-rings at the front of the saddle on the skirt and a further strap passed over the horse's wither. Sometimes, too, a further strap passed between the front legs attaching to a D-ring on the front of the cinch at one end and on to the breastplate at the other.

The modern Western saddle

With the emphasis on riding now having changed again – this time from work to pleasure riding – the Western saddle has undergone further alterations. It has been made markedly lighter by being built on a 'Ralide' synthetic tree; and by eliminating the steel reinforcements on the front arch, since this extra strength is not required for anything other than the competitive events of calf roping, for which the original heavier saddles are still available. The pommel and cantle have been lowered and the horn sloped forward and its size reduced; but it is still built so that the weight is evenly distributed over as wide an area as possible.

The flank cinch in some cases has been discarded but the modern saddles are made with a choice of three alternative cinch positions, known as $\frac{7}{8}$, $\frac{3}{4}$ or $\frac{5}{8}$ rigging, as well as centre fire rigging, and the original forward cinch position. This last position placed the rider too far back in the saddle to be ideal for today's type of riding, so the centre fire single rigging was introduced, which positioned the cinch exactly in the centre between pommel and cantle. This did not

A modern Western saddle.

Fastening a woven hair cinch by tying it to the *latigo*, i.e., 'cinching up', on a tooled Western saddle.

elaborate the design the more favoured they are, particularly for parades and carnivals which are so popular.

There are today three basic types of Western saddle: the heavier roping saddle with the reinforced arch which has a fairly flat seat with a low cantle, rounded swells and sloping horn; the cutting saddle which has a deeper seat and higher cantle with broader swells which gives greater security for fast manoeuvres; and the general-purpose saddle, which, like the English general-purpose saddle, is a compromise between the two and is ideal for trail riding and show work.

There are two further saddles reserved for the specialist activity of rodeos. These are the bronc saddle and the bareback rig. The bronc saddle is similar to the general-purpose Western saddle but its size and weight must conform to the rules laid down by the Rodeo Cowboys Association. The bareback rig is basically a strong piece of leather with no shaped seat or cantle but with stirrups and a leather handle at the pommel to hold on to. The bareback rig is held in place by centre fire rigging.

Western horse training

It was not only the Western saddles that the Spanish Conquistadores took to America; they also took a highly sophisticated system of schooling with them. It was based on a system of control using nose pressure, and employed an item called *la jaquima* to produce a highly-schooled horse. It was from *la jaquima* that we get the word 'hackamore'.

THE BOSAL HACKAMORE

The real hackamore consists of a heavy braided rawhide noseband, called a bosal, with a large knot, a heel knot, which lies under the horse's chin. It is fitted to the horse by means of a lightweight headpiece called a *latigo* which can either have a slit in it which allows it to pass over one ear, or it can be fitted with a browband, a *cavesdra*, and go over both ears in the usual way. Instead of reins, the hackamore is fitted with a rope made of horse hair which is called the *mecate*, which is attached to the heel knot by being wound round it a number of times, thus producing a finely balanced device, which together with

prove ideal either, so the other three alternatives were introduced and it is largely a matter of personal preference, taking into account the horse's conformation and the use to which he is to be put, as to whether single or double rigging is selected. In some saddles the rear rigging rings have been replaced by leather straps attached to the saddle, which has the advantage of reducing the bulk under the rider's leg, thus bringing closer contact between horse and rider. To help the rider adopt a more forward position, the seat of the saddle has less of a slope towards the cantle than of old and the stirrup is placed further back. Thus the rider can employ a slightly shorter leg position than before.

Virtually all of today's Western saddles are elaborately engraved and some in addition are mounted with silver or stainless steel, the more the rope reins, acts as a counterbalance for the noseband. The throatlatch, known as a *fiador*, is adjusted just short enough to prevent the heel knot banging against the horse's lower jaw. The bosal is basically a training bridle. In the show ring only horses under four years old may wear them.

It is just as important for the hackamore to be correctly fitted as for the English bridle; and the bosal should lie about three fingers' width below the cheekbones; but the bridle barely touches the head when no pressure is applied. When pressure is applied, however, by raising the hand, the bosal tips forward and the horse retracts his head. The amount of pressure that can be applied depends upon how many times the *mecate* is wrapped around the heel knot.

The changes of direction are made by neck reining, the rein being pulled out to the direction one wants to take while the other rein rests against the neck. When the horse has been fully schooled in the hackamore he is able to carry out sudden stops, pivots, turns and rein-backs (backing) on a loose rein.

TRAINING WITH A BIT
When the horse has reached this stage of training a bit is frequently introduced. The bit used is a curb with reasonably long cheeks and a port, the cheeks often being engraved. No bosal or other sort of noseband is used on the horse who has reached this stage of training and the reins, which are usually made of rawhide, have only the lightest contact with the mouth. The reins are, of course, carried in one hand, the loose ends being carried lightly in the free hand some 18-24 in (45-61 cm) away from the rein hand over the rider's thigh. The main paces are walk, jog and lope, all of which are smooth ground-covering paces at which the horse can travel long distances without tiring either himself or his rider. The jog is a slower pace than the trot and a

Above right: The Western bosal hackamore. It is designed to sit clear of the nose and jaw bones.

Right: Western reins are held in one hand and are left 'floating' or looping.

The trained Western horse is ridden in a light curb bit and no noseband. The weight of the reins maintains contact with the mouth.

OTHER HACKAMORES

Apart from the bosal type, the hackamore is a 'mechanical' bridle, controlling the horse without a bit by means of pressure on the poll, nose and chin groove. It has a single rein. These are some types.

The hellymore

This is useful for training and all-purpose riding. It is popular for Western riding. It has long cheeks (8 in/20 cm), fitted with curb strap loops. It is used with a curb chain. It has a leather-covered self-adjusting noseband, and pivot headstall pieces to prevent it tipping forward.

Round shank hackamore

This has round cheeks. The noseband is of leather-covered steel cable; it is movable and cannot drop over the nose. It produces the correct leverage and control while being comfortable for the horse.

Improved hackamore

This has rounded cheeks, and a noseband of braided leather over a stainless steel bicycle-type chain.

WESTERN BITS

These are two common types.

Cutting horse bit

This sometimes has a swept-back shank and sometimes a straight one, which makes for a quicker response. The mouthpiece is designed to discourage the cutting horse from bringing his head up.

Loose jaw curb bit

This has a solid copper mouthpiece to encourage saliva flow and thus prevent dryness. It is designed to avoid any pinching.

Tie-down

This is a Western-style martingale.

Western show saddlery

The most popular classes for Western horses are the Western Pleasure classes which are judged on manners, conformation and the ability of the horse to perform the walk, jog, lope and rein back, as in an ordinary showing class. Versatility classes, when the horse is first ridden in Western tack and then English tack is another popular class, as is the Trail class which is similar to a

more relaxed one, while the lope is slower than the canter and less collected.

At all paces the rider's position is a relaxed one, sitting in the deepest part of the saddle with the leg slightly bent at the knee and the lower leg hanging loosely in line with the upper part of the body. A slightly longer length of stirrup leather is employed than in English riding.

A finished Western horse in light curb bit bridle, without noseband, and open reins. Note that the reins are held in one hand only.

handy hunter competition. The Stock Horse class is designed to test the horse's ability to work cattle and he will have to demonstrate a quick start, sliding stops, flying changes and stay 'ground-tied', as well as showing that he knows how to take up and slack on a rope and hold it. Staying 'ground-tied' is an exercise in which the horse is trained to stand still when stopped and one rein is dropped to the ground, so that he appears to be tied to the ground.

For the Western Pleasure class, a Western saddle with saddle blanket is used. For novice horses a bosal hackamore or snaffle bridle is required; for others, a Western bridle with humane type Western bit and curb straps at least ½ in (1.3 cm), or a flat curb chain is needed. Split reins, bosal roping or California reins should be used. Martingales and tie-downs are not permitted.

For the Trail class, similar saddlery is used, but if a romal is used, hobbles must be carried. For the Stock Horse class it is similar again to that used in the Pleasure class, but a lariat (lassoo) must be carried and a neck rope used; if closed reins are used, hobbles must be carried.

8 Horse clothing and equipment

In addition to the actual tack the horse requires for the varied activities in which he takes part, there are a number of items of clothing and equipment which will be necessary to ensure his comfort when he is at home, and protect him from injury when he is travelling and taking part in competitions.

Headcollars (leather or nylon halters in USA)

The first piece of stable equipment that is necessary for the horse is a headcollar, (halter in USA) as it is in this that the horse will be led to and from his field, tied up for grooming, travelling etc. It consists, in essence, of a noseband, cheekpieces, headpiece and back straps, the various straps being joined together by round or square metal or brass rings, the headpiece being fastened to the cheekstraps by means of a buckle.

There are a number of headcollars on the market and a good, stout leather one is desirable. The best is made of strong cowhide with three rows of stitching along the cheek and back straps, and will have a detachable, double lined headstrap. It will also have a rolled leather throat and brass mountings and buckles, the latter, although looking very smart, making the finished item an expensive one. Cheaper variations are those with galvanized metal buckles and rings, but it is advisable to have a buckle with a groove that the tongue will not slip through; most of the cheaper headcollars fall down in this respect. Just two rows of stitching

as opposed to three, plain leather instead of rolled, and a headpiece that is not detachable will also make the headcollar cheaper, and many of this type also have adjustable nosebands. For really strong, heavy type horses a headcollar made of buffalo hide is probably the best since these are virtually unbreakable.

Recently nylon headcollars in a variety of colours have appeared on the market, and are much cheaper than leather. Some are lined in cotton to prevent chafing. The better ones have buckle adjustments at the nose and headpiece, whilst the cheaper ones have only a 'threaded through' metal fastening at the headpiece. This latter fastening is very unsatisfactory as they can and do come undone if the horse pulls back. Nylon headcollars have the advantage of being rot-proof, so do not deteriorate as much as leather ones when left on a horse living out. Metal fittings must be rustless.

For youngsters and foals a foal slip or yearling headcollar is a useful piece of equipment since there is plenty of room for adjustment, although the leather is not so strong as that used in the larger headcollars. Adjustable lightweight foal slips and headcollars are made in nylon webbing also.

Headcollars must fit properly just behind the ears and the cheekstraps hang parallel just behind the cheekbones; the noseband should be two fingers' width below the cheekbones and allow two fingers inside it. The throatlatch must prevent the headpiece going over the ears, but allow the width of a palm between it and the horse's throat.

A very much cheaper variation on the head-collar is the plain rope halter, the best form of which is the Yorkshire halter. This consists of a wide noseband sewn on to the cheek and head-piece, the latter being all in one. In addition the Yorkshire halter has a throatlatch fixed to it – a thin rope on one side which fastens on to a rope loop on the other side of the cheekpiece – which is absent in other types of halter, and this prevents the cheekpieces from being pulled over the eye. All halters incorporate a rope by which to tie the horse up or lead him. In the USA rope halters and lead ropes come separately.

Headcollars, however, require a separate rope. These should be roughly 8 ft (2.4 m) long, the best ones having a dog clip or spring clip at one end which is clipped on to the back ring of the headcollar. Other ropes have a rope loop at one end and the other end of the rope is first passed through this and then through the head-collar ring by way of attachment. The spring or dog clips can be of either brass or galvanized metal to match the fittings of the headcollar. Ropes are made in a variety of colours.

Nylon headcollars and rope halters can be cleaned by scrubbing them with soap and water, not detergent, whilst the leather headcollars are cleaned with saddle soap in the usual way and occasionally with oil or grease (*see* page 26), more often if left on horses kept out. Clips should be kept well greased if they are not to become stiff to open and close. Brass buckles can be cleaned with a proprietary brass cleaner, and polished with a soft cloth. Headcollars can be hung up when not in use on brackets or other fittings like those used for bridles, the ropes whipped up neatly.

Rugs (blankets in USA)

Most horses, if doing any degree of work during the winter months will usually be stabled, at least at night, and have their natural heavy winter coats clipped so that they do not sweat profusely thereby losing condition. In addition they are much easier to keep clean when clipped. Once their natural coat has been removed however, through having either a hunter or full clip (i.e. a hunter clip leaves the hair on the legs and the area under the saddle; the full clip re-

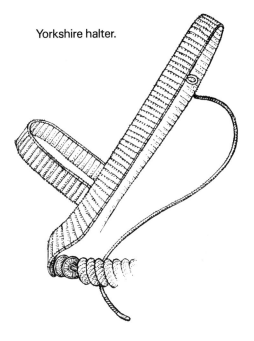

Yorkshire halter.

moves all the hair) they will need substitute clothing to keep them warm in their box (box stall) when they are not being worked or exercised.

NIGHT RUGS

The horse's first requirement will be a night rug, usually in brown or fawn, the traditional well-tried and probably the best being made of jute of various qualities or finely woven canvas, the latter being very hardwearing, with a full grey woollen mixture lining. It is a tough, utility rug, subject to strain and soiling if the horse lies down. The poor quality rugs are made of light-weight jute with only a half lining. Most jute rugs are fitted with a surcingle just behind the wither to keep them in place, as well as a strong leather strap and buckle, sometimes of blue chrome leather, at the chest.

Surcingles

These are straps which are sewn on to the rug. Most rugs (i.e. blankets) in the USA have surcingles, many of the type sewn on at an angle and crossing under the horse's belly, avoiding spine pressure.

If a surcingle is fitted to the rug care must be

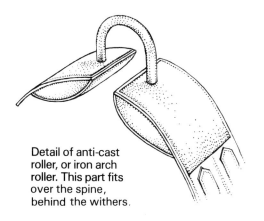

Detail of anti-cast roller, or iron arch roller. This part fits over the spine, behind the withers.

taken to ensure that it does not press on to the spine and thus cause a sore back. If there is pressure on the spine it is possible to have the surcingle padded for roughly 6 in (15 cm) either side of the spine and leave a loop over the spine itself, so that there is no constant pressure on this area. Alternatively it is possible to buy jute rugs without the surcingle attachment, in which case the rug will have to be kept in place by the use of a jute or leather roller.

Rollers (surcingles in USA)
A roller is a separate, wide strap which fastens with buckles. A rug roller differs from the breaking roller in that there is just one D-ring attachment on either side of the leather roller and the roller is made all in one piece. Jute rollers have two leather straps and buckle fastenings, the leather being attached at the bottom of the pads on the outside in the normal way. Again, care must be taken to see that the roller pads either side of the spine are kept well padded in order to avoid pressure. If an ordinary leather roller is used it is a good idea to employ a simple breastplate or breastgirth. This is a length of leather which passes across the horse's chest fastening on the roller at each side by means of a buckle fastening, and it obviates the necessity of having to fasten the roller up tightly in order to keep the rug in place.

Anti-cast rollers
One certain way to ensure that pressure is kept off the spine is to use an 'anti-cast' roller which has a leather-covered metal arch joining the pads over the spine. They are very expensive items of equipment, but in addition to avoiding pressure

they do ensure that the horse cannot roll over in his box and get cast. This happens when the horse rolls in his box (box stall) and cannot get up, either because there is insufficient space or because he is too close to a wall or door. It can be dangerous as the horse may easily panic.

Blankets
In very cold weather the horse will require a blanket under his night rug. The best are the pure new wool Witney blankets in the traditional fawn colour with black, red and blue stripes at either end, weighing about 8 lb (3.6 kg). There is also a slightly cheaper, lighter variety of blanket in all wool, as opposed to pure new wool, of similar but slightly brighter colouring. (The difference between 'pure new wool' and 'all wool' is that the former is untouched 'virgin' wool that has not been used for anything else at all, whereas the latter, although still wool, cannot be guaranteed not to have been used for another purpose and then recarded, in which case it is possible that it might contain an element of foreign matter.)

If your horse is not a particularly chilly mortal, however, an ordinary plain grey wool-and-fibre mixture army-type blanket may well be quite sufficient for him to wear under his night rug; alternatively, or in addition, he could wear an anti-sweat sheet underneath (*see* page 82).

DAY RUGS (BLANKETS IN USA)
A day rug is not essential for a stabled horse, but is an attractive item. If the horse is standing in his box (box stall) during the day and the weather is not cold enough to warrant a night rug, a day rug will look very smart. It can be used for travelling and can give a good appearance at shows with matching equipment. It is made of pure heavyweight wool (8 lb/3.6 kg) in various colours and bound with either cloth braid or livery cloth binding of a contrasting colour. It is fastened at the neck with a leather strap and buckle and has a fillet string going under the tail. It will require a roller to keep it in

Right: Day rug fastened with a fillet string and twin adjustable crossing surcingles, which avoid spine pressure.

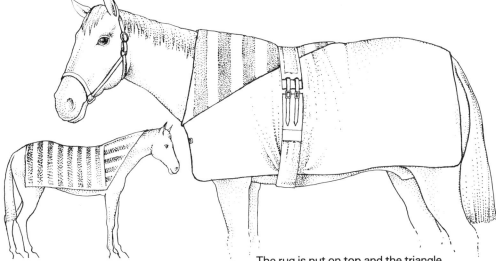

Putting on a blanket. It is put well forward up the neck, then the front corners are folded up to lie on the neck.

The rug is put on top and the triangle made by the rug at the front is folded over the front of the rug, so the roller can be fastened over the top of the blanket triangle.

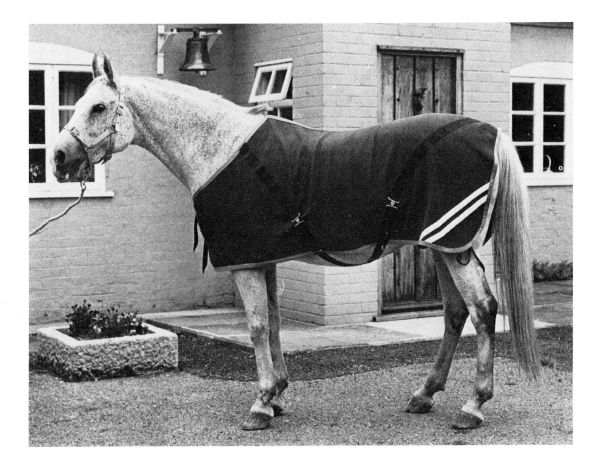

place and these can be obtained in a matching colour to the rug with either one or two straps depending upon the width. It is customary for day rugs to bear the owner's initials, in the same colour as the binding, on the back left-hand corner of the rug.

Jute rugs and woollen rugs and blankets do have to be dry-cleaned rather than washed, but canvas rugs can be scrubbed with a scrubbing brush. Wool linings of all rugs can be brushed with a stiff brush to remove the loose hairs. Rugs and blankets will benefit from being hung over the stable door to air in fine weather when the horse is being exercised.

SUMMER SHEETS

In the summer when a woollen day rug is too warm, a summer sheet worn in the stable helps to keep the coat lying flat and clean. It is therefore a virtual necessity for the show horse, especially at the show itself. It is made of cotton or linen and is of the same design as the day rug, being either of a plain colour or Tattersall check (white background with red and blue checks) with a contrasting binding. It requires a roller to keep it in place and comes with fillet strings. The owner's initials are usually put on the back left hand corner.

ANTI-SWEAT SHEETS

This is basically a cotton 'string vest' of cellular mesh, now often bound in nylon, with a buckle fastening at the chest. By creating air pockets next to the body it insulates the horse against heat or cold, so long, of course, as a rug is put on top so that the air can in fact be trapped. The anti-sweat rug's other use, of course, is to put on a horse who has sweated up, in order to help him

Checked cotton summer sheet, with roller and fillet string.

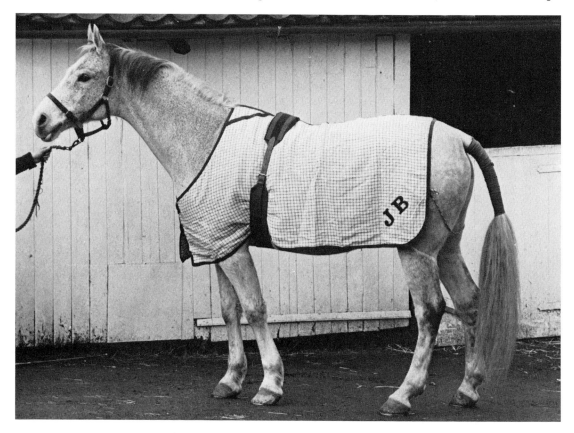

dry off without being cold – i.e. anti-sweat. It will be quite useless, however, if used (as it so frequently is) without a rug or sheet being placed on top, since the air pockets cannot then be formed. A roller is necessary to keep it in place.

The anti-sweat rug was originally known by the British manufacturers' name, Aerborne, who still produce it, although it is made by other companies also nowadays. It is available in attractive colours, besides white, and is washable.

TOWELLING RUGS (BLANKETS IN USA)
The towelling rug is an alternative to the anti-sweat sheet and serves exactly the same purpose

but does not require a sheet or rug over the top in order for the horse to dry off and keep warm. It comes in various colours and is washable.

NYLON SHEETS
The nylon sheet is made of lightweight proofed nylon with a chest fastening and fillet string. It is very useful to slip over a horse who is already saddled up, or wearing a rug, and has for some reason to stand out in the rain. It is a particularly useful piece of clothing to take to a show, for instance to slip on the horse waiting in the collecting ring if there is a sudden shower. Different colours are available and it can be wiped clean.

QUILTED AND SYNTHETIC RUGS (BLANKETS IN USA)
Although I personally favour the old and tested types of horse clothing, there have, in fairly recent times, appeared some new types of rugs

Quilted nylon rug fastened with its own attached wide surcingle with two straps.

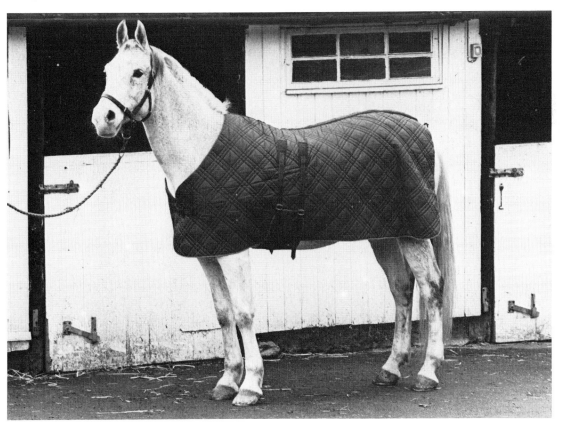

which, in most cases, appear to be perfectly satisfactory, and are certainly easier to clean.

There is, for instance, the rug based on the nylon, quilted jacket, parka and anorak. Variations on this theme are made by several firms and all are light, warm and washable, being made from quilted nylon with a polyester fibre filling and lined with either cotton (less likely to cause sweating), or brushed nylon. They are fitted with a nylon strap and metal fastenings at the chest, and some have a nylon surcingle, and frequently too they have a fillet string going under the tail to prevent the rug being displaced. If no surcingle is attached a roller will be necessary to hold the rug in place.

Another rug designed to be light, washable and very warm is that made of 'Thermatextron'. Having gone through laboratory tests Thermatextron has been shown to have a higher thermal insulation value than any other fabric and to absorb less moisture, which means that the heat generated by the horse's body is conserved, the test results estimating that the Thermatextron rug is thermally equivalent to two conventional blankets. Maximum benefit from the rug is obtained if it is worn next to the skin but it can be used instead of an anti-sweat rug to put on a wet or sweating horse, the horse drying off and staying warm without the addition of a rug on top, as the sweat evaporates through the fabric. This makes the rug very useful to put on horses who are travelling, as it will prevent them breaking out (sweating up) and getting chilled as a result, which can in due course lead to muscular problems. This rug can, too, be used in very cold weather under a night rug. It is fitted with nylon fastenings at the chest and a fillet string. Some are also fitted with crossed surcingles from the shoulder and hindquarters, crossing underneath the horse's belly and fastening with metal clips; this arrangement ensures that there is no pressure on the spine.

'Equitex' fabric is another new material to be made into night rugs and it is again washable and hardwearing. It provides ventilation as well as insulation and being lined with brushed polyester, it is warm as well. Again, it has crossed surcingle webbing fastenings to prevent spine pressure, and a patent chrome fastening at the chest.

NEW ZEALAND RUGS

If the clipped horse runs out in the paddock for a few hour's exercise each day he will need to wear, whilst he is out, a New Zealand rug. These are used on horses and ponies living out all winter, who may be trace-clipped. The New Zealand differs from the night or stable rug in that it is waterproof and windproof as well as being warm. The original waterproof rug was introduced to Britain by the Emston Saddlery Co in 1928, and although this firm has now been incorporated into Turf and Travel Ltd this same pattern rug is still made.

It is made of good quality dark fawn waterproof canvas with a heavy wool check lining and is generously cut and shaped to allow complete freedom of movement. It fits well forward over the wither and covers well over the quarters and has a drawstring round the croup which ensures that it fits snugly and does not blow up over the horse's back. It has a strong leather fastening at the front across the chest, and adjustable leather hindleg straps with spring clips which link through the hindlegs and clip back on to the metal rings of the rug. The metal rings are covered with a leather flap to ensure that they do

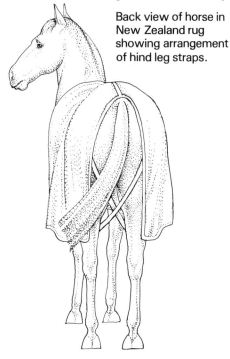

Back view of horse in New Zealand rug showing arrangement of hind leg straps.

not rub the horse's flanks. Because it is generously cut and well shaped there is no need for a surcingle to hold it in place and so back pressure is again avoided. This firm also clean and reproof their own rugs.

A similar New Zealand rug known as the 'Kiwi' works on the same principle and does not employ a surcingle but this one is made of 18 oz (510 g) flax material which is again very strong and it is lined with a 50 per cent wool blanketing. For extra protection in really bad weather, this rug also has an optional matching neck cover which buckles on to the rug at the neck and comes right up to the horse's ears, being secured by three buckles under the horse's throat.

Other New Zealand rugs, of a rather cheaper nature, are made of a slightly lesser quality canvas and because they are not so generously cut or well shaped require an attached surcingle to keep them in place. All however have the chest fastening and hindleg straps.

DUAL-PURPOSE RUGS (BLANKETS IN USA)

There are also on the market dual-purpose rugs, examples of which are the 'All Purpose' and 'Turnout' rugs, which the makers claim are suitable to double as a stable rug and a New Zealand. The 'All Purpose' rug is made from a new strong synthetic material which it is claimed is fully waterproof, all seams having been treated with a special sealant. Its feature is that it has a detachable acrylic fibre pile lining which can be clipped in and taken out by means of press studs (snaps). It is therefore warm, versatile, and is also washable.

The 'Turnout' rug known as the 'Lancer' is made in Taiwan of Oxford nylon. Although it has withstood heavy Australian rains (it is marketed in Australia) the suppliers are reluctant to

The 'Kiwi' rug, a strong type of New Zealand rug.

guarantee that it is 100 per cent waterproof, since they maintain that it is impossible to completely seal the seams. It is, however, stoutly built and 'barbed wire proof'. This again has adjustable cross surcingle straps and a chest fastening but no leg straps. It is lined with deep pile fleece and is completely washable.

There is a further 'dual purpose' rug which is marketed in the USA, known as the 'Lexington' rug, which it is claimed, is 'suitable for both stable and outdoor use'. It is made of waterproof Cordura nylon and has a fleecy lining. Again it has cross surcingles, fastenings at the chest and detachable elastic leg straps. It is washable.

The possibility of the horse sweating up under the acrylic fibre or fleecy linings of these rugs should be considered when thinking of using one.

All rugs, however, be they stable, New Zealand, day or summer sheets must fit properly to start with or they will not stay in place. The rug must be long enough, stable rugs going right up to the dock and New Zealand rugs going a little further; deep enough, and well down the flanks. They must not be too tight when fastened at the chest. Many of the cheaper rugs, and some not so cheap ones, are cut very short, the rug finishing level with the elbow and stifle respectively; but ideally they should come about 4 in (10 cm) below this level.

Most manufacturers measure their rugs from the centre of the horse's chest in a straight line round the shoulder and along the body to the horse's buttocks; but others measure their rugs from the horse's wither along the back to the top of the dock. When buying a rug do check to see what measurements are required to ensure that the rug really does fit.

When storing rugs, particularly wool ones, for any length of time, do put them away clean in a vermin proof trunk or similar container, with mothballs; otherwise when you come to use your rugs again you will find that you have more holes than rug!

BANDAGES
Leg bandages
If the weather is very cold and your horse has had a full clip he may need extra warmth on his

Above: Stable bandage fastened with Velcro on the outside of the cannon bone.

legs. In this case you will require a set of four woollen leg bandages which should be roughly 5 in (13 cm) wide and 8 ft (2.4 m) long. The traditional ones had tapes at one end for securing them in place on the outside of the cannon bone (not at the back where they will cause pressure on the tendons); but the modern ones tend to be fitted with Velcro fastenings which are quicker to take on and off and stay secured just as well.

Plain wool bandages should have Gamgee tissue (cotton wool covered with gauze) underneath them which should cover the leg from knee to coronet, the bandage being started just below the knee and extending down over the fetlock joint and tied half way up the cannon. Some woollen bandages have a short length of stockinette at either end and woollen padding in between and in this case Gamgee is not necessary. Stockinette bandages are also available although not frequently seen nowadays and these, although less warm, are perfectly satisfactory if used with Gamgee underneath. A synthetic, washable, re-usable substitute for Gamgee is available at much less cost.

It is also a good idea to apply woollen bandages with straw underneath instead of gamgee if your horse comes back wet and muddy from hunting or cross-country work, for instance; this will help to dry him off and keep him warm.

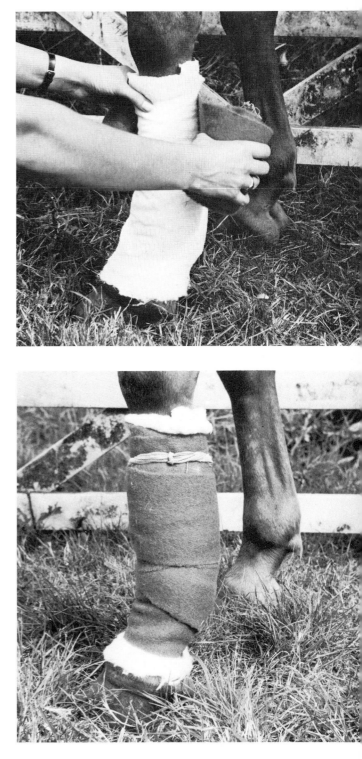

Right: Putting on a stable bandage, the Gamgee extending up to the knee and down over the coronet.

Below right: The finished stable bandage fastened with tapes on the outside of the cannon bone, the ends neatly tucked in.

Below: Woollen stable bandage with stockinette at each end; Gamgee is not necessary with this type of bandage.

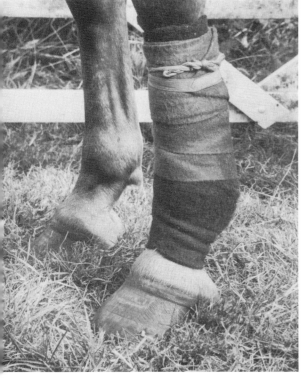

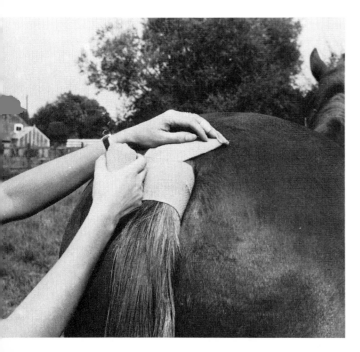

Tail bandages

The other bandage required for stable use is the tail bandage which should form part of every grooming kit. This is a long elasticated bandage which is wrapped round the tail, starting at the top and winding round the tail to the end of the dock and then half-way up again. It is tied, not too tightly, on the outside of the tail in a bow. It keeps the tail looking neat and tidy. It should not be left on overnight, since if tight enough to stay in place it will damage the tail hairs, and if tied looser will come off during the night.

Left: Putting on a tail bandage, starting at the top; the end is held in the left hand while the bandage is wrapped round with the right.

Below left: The finished tail bandage; the tapes are tied slightly looser than the bandage so circulation is not impaired.

Below: The tail guard, worn over a tail bandage and fastened to the summer sheet roller.

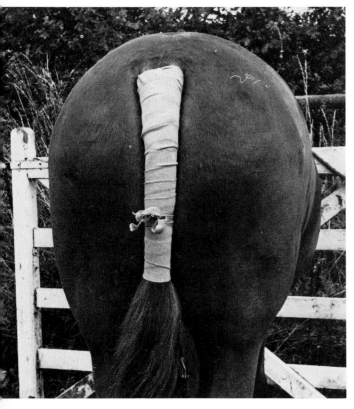

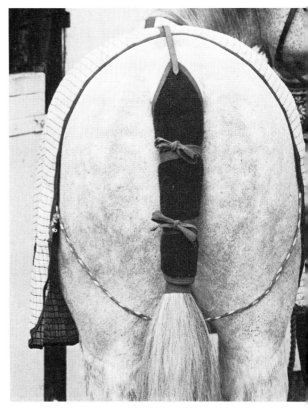

Neither should it be wetted before being put on since it is likely to shrink – the tail should be damped with a water brush before the tail bandage is applied. A tail bandage wound or tied too tightly will also restrict circulation in the dock, which must be avoided.

Bandages come in all colours and can be washed in soap and water in the ordinary way, but remember when winding them up to start at the tape or Velcro end, rolling the fastening inwards. They will then be the right way round when you come to tying them in place on the horse.

Shoe boil boot

This is used in the USA, to prevent an injury or pressure on the point of the elbow (capped elbow) caused by the shoe when the horse lies down with his foot underneath him. It is a cylindrical, stoutly-padded boot which is attached to the pastern with straps.

Travelling clothing

The horse should wear protective clothing when travelling. This will reduce the risk of him knocking himself about and damaging himself in the box (van) or trailer, which might happen if the box pulls up sharply or takes a corner a little too fast. It is also necessary to keep him warm.

The horse should be securely tied up to the ring in the trailer or box by a rope and strong headcollar.

Poll guards or head bumpers

Protection in the form of a poll guard may be necessary for the horse's head if he is inclined to carry it high or if the roof of the box is a little low for him. Poll guards (head bumpers) are made of a thick half-moon shaped piece of felt with a leather back, encompassing two slots at either end, through which the headstrap of the headcollar is passed.

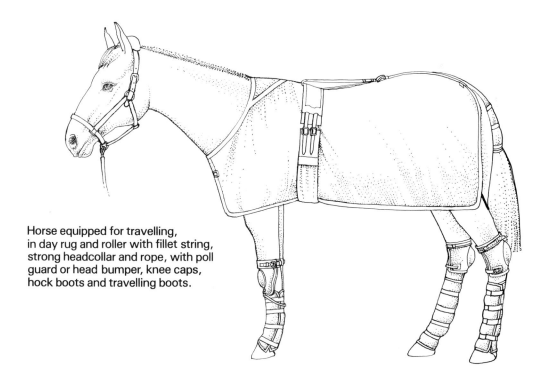

Horse equipped for travelling, in day rug and roller with fillet string, strong headcollar and rope, with poll guard or head bumper, knee caps, hock boots and travelling boots.

RUGS (BLANKETS IN USA)

Depending upon the weather he will need to wear either a summer sheet, day rug or night rug with or without a blanket underneath, and with a roller to keep it in place. For a horse being travelled home after any exertion, an anti-sweat rug with a day or night rug on top will be necessary. More rugging will be needed for a horse in a trailer than in a horse box, unless the trailer is completely enclosed at the back; and a box full of horses returning from an event will be warmer than with one horse returning from a quiet show class.

LEG PROTECTION

To prevent the legs getting knocked about stable bandages should be worn on all four legs again with the Gamgee extending up to the knee and right down over the coronet so as to give protection to the heels. Knee caps and hock boots are very useful.

Knee caps

Knee caps are a sensible way of protecting the knees from bumps, particularly if the horse should perhaps fall in the box. These consist of a strap (about 2 in/5 cm deep) of well padded leather at the top, with a thinner strap of leather sewn to it at each end, one with a buckle and the other with holes punched in it. This goes round the leg above the knee. A thick bound woollen square is sewn below this wide piece of leather. In the centre is a knee-shaped strong leather reinforcement with two straps sewn on to it at the bottom, one with a buckle, the other with punched holes. The wide leather strap buckles above the knee fairly tightly and the bottom strap buckles below the knee, loosely so as not to hamper the knee movement.

Hock boots

Horses who are likely to bump their hocks in the box will require a pair of hock boots, the best type being made of felt rather than wool. They have a strong leather reinforcement to cover the hock. There is a leather strap, preferably set on elastic at the top, and a plain leather one at the bottom, the latter being fastened loosely so as not to interfere with the hock movement.

All-in-one travelling boots

There are on the market horse and pony leg protectors which obviate the necessity for ban-

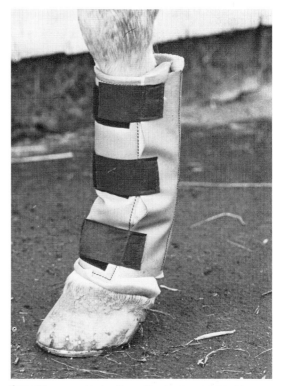

One of the many kinds of travelling boots available. These have a foam rubber padding inside, are plastic outside and have Velcro fastenings.

dages and either knee or hock boots. An example available in Britain are 'Limbuffs'. They are made of a nylon-reinforced PVC outer covering with a non-absorbent fur fabric lining, and have reinforcements over the knee and hock areas. They are knee caps, or hock boots, plus protectors for the cannon, fetlock, pastern, coronet, heel and hoof wall all in one. They are fastened with Velcro above the knee and have a further three Velcro fastenings at the back of the tendon and fetlock. They are washable and easy to put on and take off. In the USA there are shipping boots which serve this purpose, made of foam rubber cased in terry.

TAIL PROTECTION

The horse should also wear a tail bandage to keep his tail tidy and stop it being rubbed by the back of the trailer.

Tail guards

Some horses really lean on the trailer ramp and scrub their tails against it, in which case a tail guard is a sensible protection for them to wear. This is a rectangular-shaped piece of equipment made of either leather, canvas or wool. Leather ones have three buckle arrangements, and the canvas and wool ones fasten with three tapes which are sewn on. These fasten round the tail over the tail bandage, tieing or buckling up on the outside. At the top of the guard is a long leather strap which lies from the top of the tail along the back of the horse, goes under the arch of the roller and buckles back on to itself to keep the tail guard in place.

Exercise and working clothing

EXERCISE OR QUARTER SHEETS

If you are exercising a Thoroughbred-type horse on a particularly cold day just after he has been clipped out, he might require an exercise sheet to keep him warm. Exercise sheets are made of the same fawn striped wool blanketing as under-blankets, and are bound with cloth binding. They are worn under the saddle, the front edges being turned back and secured by the girth under the saddle flap. The sheet stretches back just far enough to cover the loins.

EXERCISE BANDAGES

A number of horses tend to throw their legs about a bit when being ridden and, therefore, need to have their legs protected against any blows or injuries. Unfit horses or those doing competitive work will also benefit from wearing exercise bandages to give support to the tendons. Exercise bandages are the same as tail bandages, being made of elasticated stretchy material. These should be applied, over gamgee, to either both fore or both hind legs, or all four legs wherever it is felt support is needed. Exercise bandages are applied below the knee and are wound down as far as the bottom of the cannon but above the fetlock joint, clockwise on near-side legs, anti-clockwise on off-side legs; and should be tied fairly tightly on the outside of the cannon.

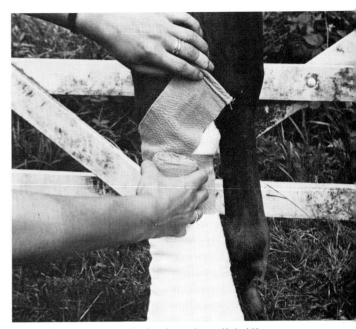

Above: Putting on an exercise bandage; the end is held in the left hand then folded down and covered.

Below: The finished exercise bandage, reaching from below knee or hock to fetlock.

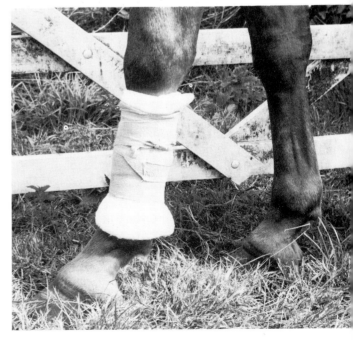

91

Horses wearing exercise bandages for show-jumping, hunting or cross-country work should have the bandages sewn on after the tapes have been tied. This should prevent them coming undone and the horse catching his legs in them, perhaps being brought down as a result. As an added precaution against this happening during a fast competitive cross-country event it is a good idea to wind wide sticky waterproof elastoplast over the bandage after it has been sewn. This will also help to stop the bandage getting too wet and muddy, and give even greater support to the tendons.

BOOTS

There are a number of boots on the market designed to protect the legs from common injuries caused by brushing, over-reaching, speedy-cutting etc, or to youngsters being schooled on the flat and over fixed fences.

Brushing boots

Brushing occurs when a horse knocks his foot against the inside of the opposite leg, usually round the fetlock joint. Sometimes this is caused by incorrect action due to faulty shoeing, in which case corrective shoeing can put the matter right; failing that, one of the various types of brushing boots will give protection. The simplest is the Yorkshire boot, which is less popular today than in the past. It is an oblong piece of felt with a tape sewn along the centre which is tied just above the fetlock joint; the felt above the tape is then doubled over to give added protection. Another simple brushing boot consists of a spectacle-shaped piece of felt with leather reinforcements over the side of the fetlock and a leather strap which fastens round the back of the fetlock or at the side. A further short, simple type of boot consists of an oval-shaped piece of felt, with a leather strap and buckle fastening at the top which straps above the fetlock, and with a shaped leather extension which fits over the fetlock joint on the inside.

A longer brushing boot is also available which fits along the cannon bone. It is made of cloth or leather with a shaped leather reinforcement to cover the fetlock area, being kept in place by four or five leather straps and buckles. Since it gives a degree of support to the tendon, it can be worn instead of bandages. Recently long

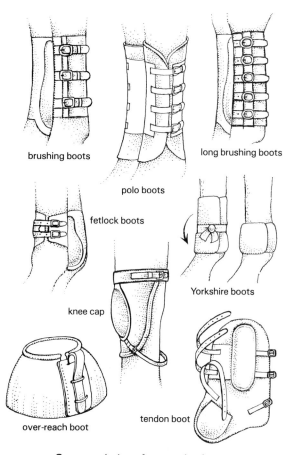

brushing boots
long brushing boots
polo boots
fetlock boots
knee cap
Yorkshire boots
over-reach boot
tendon boot

Some varieties of protective boots.

brushing boots made of strong plastic and nylon, with a textured lining, have appeared on the market. They are kept in place by three metal clip fastenings, their advantage being that they are very tough and easy to keep clean, just requiring a wipe over.

Over-reach or bell boots

Many showjumpers wear over-reach boots, since a common injury sustained by jumpers occurs when the hind shoe catches on or just above the heel of the fore foot when landing over a jump. If this happens, rubber over-reach boots provide protection from heel injury. There are two types of over-reach boots, the ordinary grooved circular rubber ones with plain rubber at the top; and those with an opening down one side, at one edge of which are three metal D-rings, while on the other edge is a leather strap which slots through the D-rings. This latter type are, of course, easier to put on and take off, whereas the plain circular ones can be a bit difficult to pull over a large hoof. The rubber does, however, provide a degree of elasticity and the boots should fit fairly tightly.

Tendon boots

Should the horse over-reach higher up the leg above the fetlock joint (i.e. speedycutting) there is a strong possibility that the tendon can be damaged. If there is a possibility of this a tendon boot should be fitted. These are made of leather, box cloth or strong woollen, Kersey, or more recently PVC material, and are well padded at the rear thus affording considerable protection to the tendons as well as giving extra support for weak tendons. They have four buckle or Velcro fastenings to keep them in place.

There are also perforated cushioned tendon protectors for use underneath exercise bandages; and lightweight tendon protectors to be used independently, of cushioned material partly covered by hard plastic, fastened with elastic Velcro straps. They are useful for showjumping, lungeing, schooling, travelling and exercise, and are washable.

Speedycutting boots are very similar to the longer brushing boots but are made of leather and also have padding at the rear.

All leather boots will need to be kept clean by washing and using saddle soap in the usual way. Felt boots need regular brushing if they are to be kept soft and free from mud. Both leather and felt boots do tend to get very wet and muddy and take a long time to dry. Rubber over-reach boots should have the mud washed off and be allowed to dry away from direct heat.

Schooling boots

There are many varieties of schooling boots, the strongest being polo boots, made of leather backed with felt. There are however a number of boots of similar design made of plastic, PVC or rubber covered with nylon, all of which have Velcro fastenings. Different manufacturers produce slightly different boots but all follow the same basic design.

Skeleton knee caps

One further leg protection that might be of benefit, particularly to youngsters being schooled over fixed fences or being ridden on the roads, is the skeleton knee cap. This is the same as the ordinary knee cap but without the woollen cloth attachment. It prevents the horse from injuring himself by bumping his knees on solid timber poles. For youngsters being ridden on the roads it will prevent any injury from broken knees (i.e. when the horse falls, as a result perhaps of spooking, and grazes his knees, a deep graze resulting in white hairs coming through when the hair grows over the area again.

Care should be taken when putting either bandages or boots with Velcro fittings on a young horse, since the unaccustomed noise may initially upset him.

'Equiboots' or 'Easyboots'

These are a fairly new type of protective boot for the hoof, made of tough synthetic material with a firm metal clip fastening. They are used when the hoof is damaged and for rough or slippery going. Shoes are not worn with these boots.

Glossary

Terms not explained here may be found in Index.

Above the bit Describes a horse which raises and stretches his head forward with his mouth higher than the rider's hand.

Bars of mouth The gap in the lower jaw between the molar and incisor teeth or tushes where the bit lies in the mouth.

Behind the bit Describes a horse which draws his head back away from contact with the bit, thus evading its action i.e. overbent.

Black saddler Term applied to a maker of driving harness as opposed to riding tack.

Brown saddler Term applied to a maker of saddles and bridles as opposed to driving harness.

Butt That part of the cattle hide, i.e. its back, which is the most suitable for the making of saddlery.

Cheeks (also known as shanks) The arms of the bit, such as a Weymouth or Hackamore, which can be of various lengths to achieve greater or lesser leverage.

Cheekpieces Bridle straps to which bit attaches.

Collection State wherein the horse, by engaging his hindquarters, has his head positioned just in front of the vertical and moves forward in a free yet contained fashion.

Contact The connection between the rider's hand and the horse's mouth through the reins. Contact should be light but firm, the degree depending on the stage of the horse's schooling.

Curb groove The groove just behind the horse's chin in front of the lower jaw bones.

Direct Rein (also known as the opening rein) This is used by the rider opening the rein in the direction in which he wants the horse to move.

Engaging the hocks (also known as getting hocks well under) When the hind legs advance well under the body and the haunches are lowered through flexion of the stifle and hocks.

Foaling slip (Dutch slip) Foal's light leather or web headcollar, adjustable at throat, nose and head, with short strap at back.

Forehand Collectively describes head, neck, withers, shoulders and forelegs of horse.

Gall Sore place usually caused by badly fitting tack, frequently under girth or saddle, i.e. girth gall, saddle gall.

Good mouth Wet mouth, the horse having made saliva by 'mouthing' the bit.

Havana colour Mid-brown saddlery colour darker than London and lighter than Warwick colour.

Head carriage The position of the horse's head.

High school airs (also known as airs above the ground) Those movements performed with either the fore, hind or all four feet off the ground. They are: the *Levade* (the horse raises his fore feet off the ground and draws them in while the lowered hind quarters bear the body's weight); *Courbette* (the horse rears and jumps forward on bent hocks); *Ballotade* (the horse bends his knees and raises his quarters almost vertically); *Croupade* (almost the same as the *Ballotade*); *Capriole* (the horse half rears and with very flexed hocks jumps forward and up in the air, then kicks out with his hindlegs).

Hollow back Opposite of roach back; a concave outline, often seen in old horses when it is an indication of age.

Independent seat That of educated and practised rider able to ride in balance with horse independent of reins and stirrups.

Indirect rein Opposite of direct rein and used against the opposite side of the neck to the direction in which the horse is required to move.

London colour Light golden brown saddlery colour.

Loriner One who makes bits, stirrups, spurs and other metal saddlery items.

Lungeing Used in the initial stages of training when lunge line is attached to cavesson headcollar, and the trainer circles horse round him at walk, trot, canter and halt, and teaches obedience to the voice.

Manège Marked-out enclosure for the teaching of horses and riders.

Near side The left hand side of the horse.

Off side The right hand side of the horse.

Overbent Describes the horse's head when positioned beyond the vertical towards the chest.

Port High or low arc in mouthpiece centre of straight bar bit; the higher the port the greater the bit's severity.

Roach back Conformational defect of the horse's back giving the back a convex appearance. It presents problems when fitting a saddle.

Roller Length of leather or webbing with pads either side of the spine and one or two buckle fastenings. It is placed over a day or night rug to keep the rug in place.

Saddle furniture Collectively describes stirrups, leathers, girth and buckle guards.

Sprain Severe strain; may be due to uncoordinated movement in rutted going or sudden extra effort by tired or unfit horse.

Strain Stretched or pulled muscle or ligament.

Surcingle Wide hemp, jute or synthetic strap; usually sewn on to night rug, and buckled to keep it in place; web ones are used over racing and eventing saddles for security.

Topline Term used to describe the shape of the horse from wither to croup. A nicely rounded slightly convex topline should be aimed at.

Warwick colour Very dark brown saddlery colour.

Weight cloth Cloth made of leather and felt with pockets on either side into which lead is inserted for increased weight for eventing and racing. It is placed on the horse's back under the saddle.

Index